Ganterbury
Tales
An Alphabetical Trip Through
Four Decades Following
Sunderland Away From Home

By Sobs & Pos

Copyright © ALS Publications
First Published in 2010

Written By Sobs & Pos

ISBN 978-0-9560846-4-4

Design & Layout: Paul Forrest (*www.alsdesign.co.uk*)
Production Editor: Martyn McFadden
Picture Editor: Chris Fryatt
Proof Reading: Sheila Seacroft & Andy Fury

www.a-love-supreme.com

For Linda, Nikki, and Kris...

With thanks to Judith, Gary, and Ian...

... and remembering Derek Poskett, Dave Raine, Bernard James, and Stephen Wilson, all of whom took part in at least some of the events portrayed in this book.

That's Pos, Reg, Bernie, and Squinny to you and me.
They Kept the Faith.

Gary Rowell
Strokes in the third goal of a memorable hat trick to see
off Newcastle 4-1 away from home in February 1979.

F oreword

I've always thought that there's a fine line between blind loyalty and insanity when it comes to football fans and in particular those who travel to follow their teams away from home.

One trophy in forty years of loyal support and thousands of miles travelled doesn't seem like a fair return for all the effort and expense that Sunderland fans have put in over those years, but that would be missing the point.

There's a great pride in following your team the length and breadth of the country. An away win is celebrated in style, with great joy and enthusiasm and even the worst defeats are treated as a badge of honour and often with a fair bit of gallows humour.

It has been my great fortune to play for Sunderland in front of these people and to experience the incredible passion they generate is something you never forget.

One of my earliest games for SAFC was away to Hull City, at the old Boothferry Park, in the seventies. As I ran out all I could see was Red and White. Sunderland fans filled three sides of the ground and the noise was deafening. It was simply unbelievable.

But that wasn't a one off. I've lost count of the number of times that we've gone away and taken over a ground, both vocally and in numbers and if there's a better away following than Sunderland's I've yet to see it.

Having read and enjoyed Sobs' first book, Keep The Faith, I was looking forward to his follow up and I'm glad to report that Ganterbury Tales is a celebration of our unique support and the many daft stories and happenings that occur on a typical SAFC awayday.

Gary Rowell

# **I**ntroduction

Long ago, in a public house not that far, far, away, my mate Pos and I were talking garbage about football, as we tended to do when we got together and we had a pint in our hands. Actually, it was in the Saltgrass before a match, and it was at the back end of the last millennium. On our way to the match, we'd read a story in A Love Supreme which described the fun and games that a group of lads had enjoyed as they travelled to an away game as daft youngsters some twenty-odd years before. Just our vintage, we reckoned, and we carried on talking garbage about football, coming to the conclusion that if you changed the names and the pick-up points, it could have been us in that story.

As we talked further, it became apparent that we had a daft story for just about every away game that we'd been to, and that it might be a bit of an idea to write them down before they disappeared into the mists of time and dead brain cells. Thankfully, we were both blessed with a ridiculously detailed recollection of what went on in those halcyon days of Oxford Bags, red and white Tams, Fulwell Enders, tartan scarves, Levi jackets done up with only the second button from the top, and very shiny footwear with lots of lace-holes – not to mention footballers with sideburns you could hide a pair of badgers in, and buses so ancient that horses and pedal cycles overtook them.

The thing with away games is that, for most fans and most matches, it's much more of an effort to get there, so folks tend to make a special effort to enjoy themselves. While there have been plenty of non-football moments at home games to put a smile on your face, such as poor David Ginola's attempt to remove the dripping remains of a pie from his hair at Roker Park, they seem to be accentuated when away from home. Would young Robert have fallen asleep in the lavvies at Roker or the SOL until the wee small hours? I doubt it, but the Amsterdam Arena in 2009 was part of such a mind-boggling trip that he not only snoozed away the second half of our game against Benfica, but right through ninety minutes of the following game between Atletico Madrid and Ajax. He'd have been there when we returned on the Sunday to play Atletico had his snores not alerted the security patrol at 2am. Travelling away with Sunderland makes you daft, it's official.

Travelling to home games, for most folks, involves a shorter journey and thus less time and opportunity to get involved in mischief. We've all managed to make the most of that opportunity, mind – get straight onto the top deck, cover the driver's periscope with a Levi jacket, and let the mischief commence. We've tied a mate to a seat on the top deck of the OK special using his own scarf on the way back from Roker, and then waited well into the night for him to be released from the OK garage. We incurred the wrath of the driver, on one memorable occasion causing the bus to be stopped and the driver to rush upstairs and threaten to hoy us off if we didn't "get squared round". We've opened sneaky bottles of beer using our shoes or the old cigarette stubbers you used to get on the back of the seats, and we even saw a marriage consummated in the Fulwell during a game, champagne all round... so home games were fun, but away games offered more. We've had buses that have broken down, meaning two sets of passengers on one bus, cosy as you like. We've had buses that broke down, and limped from Scotch Corner to Manchester with no suspension on one side, we've had the windscreen wipers cease to function in a thunderstorm. We've had buses turn up with the card tables still in place and the seats set out like a train carriage – nice, but not enough seats. We've had the bus toilet catch fire on the way back from West Ham, and we've had people locked in the bus toilet. We've had cars fill up with rainwater, or break down on the way to away games and be abandoned with the hapless driver left to stand guard – it was his car, and therefore his fault, after all.

"If we're talking about travelling, we should call it Ganterbury Tales," said Pos, and off we went to the match with a promise to meet up back in Bishop that night, armed with nothing more than our memories, a notebook and pen, and a thirst sufficient to sustain us in our first evening's ramblings. Our extensive knowledge of the English alphabet allowed us to arrange our tales in order from A to Z, and we were certain that most travellers to away games would recognise situations, games, and places that would be, if not exactly the same as those they experienced, close enough to their own experiences as to bring back a load of memories. Once we started, we agreed that we should carry on keeping a record of our travels, as many clubs had moved grounds purely in order to allow us to expand our travelling experience. We had got a decent amount of stories done when Pos suddenly and sadly passed away back in 2002, and I decided that I should carry on committing our daft experiences to magnetic memory, which had replaced paper by the time we had got going. I also decided that it shouldn't end there, and have kept records of my travels since then. As it was a joint venture, you'll find that some tales are written from the perspective of Pos, and others from my perspective, but the same people were involved in most of the antics, so it would have been wrong to change them or leave any out. We'd started our Sunderland supporting careers at the same time, started travelling to away games at the same time, and spent an inordinate amount of time at school planning Sunderland trips, so, like lots of other folks down the years, we'd sort of grown up following the Lads.

Some of the grounds are now better, most are safer, and others seem to have replaced their predecessor's atmosphere with ambience, but, most importantly, they stage football matches and Sunderland play in them. No matter how many years we've been travelling, following Sunderland always seems to come up trumps when it comes to having a good day out, so the stories just keep coming. So here goes – an alphabetical tour of football spanning forty years.

Is For Arsenal

There have been many visits to the marbled halls of Highbury throughout the history of Sunderland, and many during my time travelling with the Lads. It has carried on in the years since Highbury's demise, with Ashburton Grove, or the Emirates – call it what you will – now the destination.

In my time, apart from some scattered draws and two consecutive league wins in May and November 1983, it's been a journey that brought little, if any, joy. There was also a memorable League Cup win in 2003, our reserves coming from two goals down to beat their reserves 3-2. Thanks to my inability to let things lie with an over-exuberant member of the constabulary who decided that having a good time and celebrating our first goal was an ejectable offence, I spent the last half hour outside trying to get back in. So to date I've never actually seen us win there, and I don't even have my ticket from the game I went to when we did win – if you read the very small print, apparently, it states that tickets at all times remain the property of the club, and, in the event of your being hoyed out, the police become representatives of said club, and can take them off you. Anyhow, for some reason, just as Chelsea or Spurs have always seemed to be the least popular of London clubs for us Mackems to visit, Arsenal has always seemed to be the trip to the capital that Wearsiders put ahead of the others. Maybe it's the proximity to King's Cross – an even shorter tube ride now that they've moved grounds – or maybe it's that Grand Old Arsenal thing, the history, the manner in which the club has been run. Who knows, but whatever it is, it makes the tickets for this fixture very popular, particularly amongst exiles in the South East who can't get to many games.

My little group of travellers, the self-proclaimed ICPP (the first two letters stand for Inter City and the fourth for Pots, so you can work out the third, and we're probably one of several groups to have named themselves thus) have always made an effort to make a big day of Arsenal trips. Since the Lamb was discovered way back in 1980 during a tour of London's fleshpots ahead of a mate's wedding, it has been the destination of choice when heading to Arsenal. Ten minutes' stroll from King's Cross, a couple of stops from there to the match after lunchtime lubrication, it's been the location of many a happy pre-match congregation of red and whites over the years. In fact, just arrive there before an Arsenal Sunderland game, and I'll guarantee you'll find someone I went to school with, plus others from around the land (Colchester and Rutland spring to mind – lads with the same taste in football and pubs who are now met with whenever we play in the South East), with Sunderland on their minds. I'm not telling you the exact address, because it's ours and we want to keep it to ourselves, but if you like that sort of place you'll know it anyway. The ICPP have had numerous memorable days in the Lamb. It's just a shame that so many of the games have meant a full-on wake there before dashing back for the train home.

In a footballing sense, the fixture in September 1996 was a disaster, as the brave resistance of the nine was no match for the 11 internationals and the referee. Peter Reid was trying to steady the ship he'd guided ahead of schedule to the promised land of the Premier League, and a trip to Arsenal for our eighth match of the season was always going to be more than a wee bit tricky.

Off the field, we had the usual memorable day. Piling off the train full of pies and unsubstantiated optimism, we decided that this was the day the Lads would get one over on Arsenal and surprise the football world with a display of attacking verve and total football that would leave the Gunners shell-shocked and defeated. We had our usual daft bets on the first scorer (Ball, Scott, and Ord) at King's Cross, when Frankie Dettori would have brought us about £750,000 for the same outlay as he rode seven winners at Ascot – and he's an Arsenal fan. We should have known that would happen. As we were well ahead of pub opening time, breakfast was at Del's Diner – which had the same staff and cutlery as on our first visit on cup final day in '73. Beneath the arches outside St Pancras station, this splendid hostelry had toilet paper for serviettes, and a bog door that opened straight into the eating area. Not only that, but it wouldn't lock or even close, and was too far away to hold shut. This meant that the only way privacy could be obtained was by standing on one leg with the other at 90 degrees behind you (if you were nine feet tall). Suffice to say number twos were out of the question. We had a waiter who resembled a paler version of Sammy Davis

Junior's uglier and skinnier brother, who had the fattest cockney accent outside of Walford but told us that he came from Wallsend. The food was cheap (I should bloody well have hoped so), plentiful, and good, providing you didn't watch the preparation too closely, as everything was fried on one big hotplate with little cake-rings around the fried eggs - presumably to prevent them making a bid for freedom. We jokingly asked for a plate, but Sammy's kid brother took it all in good heart. I know it sounds pretty unappetising, but that sort of food sets you up perfectly for football and, prior to that, the next part of the day's preparations - the liquid part.

Del's Diner had since transformed into Cafe Shiraz, and served toast instead of fried bread. We blamed New Labour for that unwelcome transformation, at the same time giving praise where praise was due for seeing that the lavvy door got mended. Since that transformation, St Pancras has itself transformed, the arches are no longer home to greasy spoon cafes, taxi offices, and gentlemen's hairdressers, and Del's Diner/Café Shiraz is no more, its space in the world now occupied by the storeroom of one of the "retail outlets" that populate the semi-underground shopping mall-cum-ticket office beneath the steps of the station. Just a few memories amongst the many that go to make up the football experience, that's all that's left. Maybe Sammy's brother went back to Wallsend and opened up a Greasy Spoon on Scrogg Road. Maybe he didn't.

The Lamb in Holborn (Oops, nearly gave it away there) was where we met the remainder of our party, who had travelled from as far afield as London, Bradford, Shildon, Cheshire, and Gloustershire, and some had spent the morning in the National Gallery at an exhibition of paintings by Cheetah, the chimp from the Tarzan films (honest, and they wore the badges all day to prove it). We even had an Arsenal supporter in the considerable shape of Mike Amos of the Northern Echo, who tried his best to out-sing the other dozen of us, but even his formidable baritone stood no chance. Stubber, having travelled from Bradford, wanted a photographic record of his day out, but left his camera in the pub when he nipped out early for a look around the ground, and found some interesting shots when he eventually had the film processed (guilty, mate - sorry!) which I doubt he added to the family album.

Remember that daft bet? We'd put it on before having a drink and it seemed less daft after a few pints, but in reality our line-up should have brought us crashing back to sobriety and reality. Apart from Dickie Ord not even being in the squad, thus reducing our chances of a financial return by one third before a ball was even kicked, there was the team on the field to consider. Tony Coton was making his tenth consecutive appearance since arriving from Manchester United, and only two games away from the broken leg at Southampton that would effectively finish his career. In front of him, Gareth Hall and Scotty joined Bally and Melville in defence, and the midfield of Bracewell, Mickey Gray, Agnew and Alex Rae backed up the front two of Lee Howey and Paul Stewart. Frightening when you look back, really, but these were the boys we believed in back then, and if truth be told, they didn't really acquit themselves that badly, all things considered. Arsenal, boasting the likes of Bergkamp, Seaman, Bould, Adams, Parlour, Keown, Wright, Dixon, Winterburn – shall I stop there? - came at us, we bit back and actually knocked the ball about a bit, but then things went downhill faster than a Mag heading for Greggs. Future Sunderland player Steve Bould clattered into the back of Paul Stewart, who hit the ball with his hand on his way to the turf, and got sent off. Scotty put in his second boisterous tackle of the day and got sent off. Reidy understandably lost his rag and was sent to the stands, presumably so that he couldn't reach the referee to stick his whistle where the sun don't shine. Those left on the pitch donned their tin hats, dug their trenches, and did a passing impersonation of Michael Caine and company at Rorke's Drift. Gray and Agnew were reduced to hoofing the ball to the corner flags, Bridges replaced Bracewell – who was booked and thus likely to be sent off as well – Kubicki came on for Mad Alex, and Craig Russell for Gray. Big Chief Lee Howey gave up being a forward and joined the defence – at least that way he got to see something of the ball. It was football murder, and it is rumoured that this was the day that the last of Agnew's hair vanished. We scarcely crossed into Arsenal's half after the break, which at least meant the visiting fans had the ball at their end for 45 minutes. As on that famous occasion in Africa in 1879, those wearing red triumphed in the end, with two late goals. Just to spoil our day out.

If the football was a little disappointing, the officiating of it was even more so. There was less chance of us getting anything out of the game than us flying back to the North East in a Zeppelin. On the hour mark, the two Petes escape by battering on the gates until the steward decided that the cost of repair was more than his job was worth, and let them out. By the time we got back to the Lamb, they were well down a barrel of Winter Warmer (a well known light session beer, about 6% ABV), and took a bit of shifting to catch the train.

A lightning raid of the offy adjacent to the station, as Big Pete dished out the orders – "Poskett and Dobson, offy, beer. We'll get pies" - and we were stocked up and on our way home, treating the non-football passengers to a medley of Sunderland songs from the sixties and seventies - who can forget favourites like "hi ho, hi ho, we're off to Mexico, with Colin Todd and the Engerland squad, hi ho, hi ho"? This singing continued unabated to Darlington, although the bit after Peterborough was a bit of a blur. What is it with Peterborough? On a football train journey, it always signals something – buffet car closed on the way down, buffet car closed on the way back, unruly element ejected on the way back, the list is endless. We do, however, absolutely deny using obscene language at any time, and it wasn't one of us who dropped his keks and caused the next London trip to be a dry one. Sorry lads, we're not rude, just severely musically challenged. We didn't sing in the taxi across Darlo, but we were asked to stop singing in the Number 22 pub - admittedly, we were a little out of tune by then, and didn't quite fit the image of the typical customer. On the last leg of the journey, we howled with laughter as one of our party slid the full length of the upper deck on his back when the service bus stopped sharply at Shildon, and it is alleged that we had further beers in Bishop. I'm still not convinced about that one, although experience tells me that it is probably true.

A good day out spoiled by the 90 minutes in the middle, but our motto is and always has been "never let the deficiencies on the field spoil the fun off it." Let's get that one straight before we move any further into the alphabet.

 **Is For Barnsley**

Maybe I'm being a little bit guilty of imagining the stereotypical here, but when thinking of Barnsley, I always expect to bump into Michael Palin wearing a huge flat cap, standing outside a tiny back-to–back terrace house, the cobbled back lane festooned with washing, seventeen children screaming on the step, all the while thumbing his pocket-watch while chewing on a barm-cake and kicking his whippet. In reality, it's not that bad, having given us Jeff Clarke and my mate Burnsy, but for a long time it was like going back in time to the depression of the 1930s.

A decade or so ago, the attitude of the locals was also typically of the well-balanced Yorkshire variety (large chip on each shoulder), so we would avoid the town centre if at all possible. I did try once, but a tiny flash of red and white stripes on a badge I'd forgotten adorned my jacket, and someone on the pub door – maybe a bouncer, maybe just Seth from Fitzwilliam – informed me that it was home fans only. In reality, it's always been a good trip, not least because of its relatively close proximity to the North East. In two hours, on a bad day, you could be down the A1/M1 and be shouting "Ayuuup" with the best of them. Hence the inevitability of a large turnout, and the guarantee of locals standing at their gates, arms folded Les Dawson style, commenting to their neighbours on the size and sound of the visitors, while their many and scruffy offspring pointed from their bedroom windows in awe at the number of buses rumbling, wagon train-like, down the road to the ground. The place hasn't been that bad to us results-wise in recent years – who could forget the snowy evening in April 1999 as we triumphed 3-1 to take the Championship in record breaking style? The club, or rather their manager, was good to me a few years back, when as they went on their famous FA Cup run, we threatened to overrun the ground and were well short of tickets. The gaffer at the time is a cousin of a mate (everybody should have at least one) and he came up trumps with a small brown envelope to be collected, completely legitimately, at the ticket office. The bloke deserves better than the grief he's getting in South West Durham for resigning his Darlington job by email, or maybe he does deserve it, but we all got seats, and everybody was happy.

Due to that perceived lack of hospitality in the town – how much money was denied the local economy by the powers that be deciding that the pubs and clubs should not be allowed to open before several games? - we always drink outside of the town, be it Wakefield or somewhere equally fortunate. Way back in April 1990, we were moving through the league nicely in a season that would end in controversial fashion as we lost the Play Off Final to Swindon but were promoted due to their lack of financial sense. As a bonus, we had beaten the Mags in the semi-final after finishing sixth to their third – but you already know that didn't you? We needed something from the game to keep our promotion push on the rails. Bearing in mind the likely lack of refreshment facilities in the town, we decided on this occasion to try a pub called the Old Post Office that I had found in the Good Beer Guide. It was supposed to be next the motorway junction, ten minutes up the road before Barnsley. We duly scoured the neighbouring villages without success, and turned back to the M1 amidst threats from Skinner about where he would put my Good Beer Guide once he'd finished rolling it up. On arriving back at the junction, we found the Old Post Office, one hundred yards from the motorway. Boy, was I popular, but when we got in we found it was fine, with a good choice of bevvy, and some nice scran in the form of those giant Yorkshire puddings full of mince. They didn't appreciate our colourful language, and the landlord at one stage commented that "we'll be going our separate ways shortly." Skinner's question in reply – "why, are you going on holiday, like?" seemed to break the ice, and our continued presence was only guaranteed after some protracted negotiations and the promise that we would whistle rather than sing for the rest of our stay.

The excellent brews of Yorkshire had set us up nicely for a good match, but we didn't get it, largely thanks to a bald gentleman who ran the midfield for the Tykes, and scored the only goal. I said there and then we should buy him, so we did. Trouble was, it was not until five years later that Mr Agnew eventually signed, by which time he'd been to Blackburn and Leicester, and we'd arguably missed his best years. Typical. Agernew, Agernew, Stevie Agernew, he's got no hair, but we don't care, Stevie Agernew. Our team was largely that which turned out at Wembley shortly afterwards, with Norman, Kay, Hardyman, Bracewell, McPhail, Owers, Armstrong, Gabbiadini, and Pascoe being the well-known names, the only anomalies being Micky Heathcote, playing the 13th of his 17 games for Sunderland – we'd scored seven in each of his first two games, so he must have thought he was on to a good thing – and Kieron Brady. Even his undoubted wizardry couldn't save us, nor could the experience of his replacement, Gates. Typically for Sunderland, it was yet another disappointment for a particularly large travelling group of fans. The high point of the game was the Sunderland fans humming the Hovis theme at the home fans. It sums the place up perfectly, but you can understand the locals getting a bit sick of that sort of thing.

I went to our next game at Barnsley, and headed for the Old Post Office again. You couldn't get parked within half a mile of the place, as it was the midweek disco. When we eventually got in, we found it was the place where everyone in South Yorkshire took other people's wives (presumably while their husbands were at the football), and, as four lads on our own, were viewed as potential opposition by the local male population. We assured them that we were only there for the beer and the football.

Approaching the ground from the daft little car park up the hill was like being in the middle of a cattle stampede – thousands of feet raised a thick cloud of red dust from the dirt road to the away end, and the usual pre-match songs were interspersed with cries of "Rawhide" and "Giddyup". On this occasion, the football matched the beer, and, on a brilliantly sunny early season evening, we tore them to shreds and won 3-0 thanks to Owers, Armstrong, and substitute Pascoe. He'd come on for Thomas Hauser, who'd done all sorts in the penalty box without looking like he would score a goal, but caused enough havoc to allow others to benefit. In all honesty, it could have been ten, but we were happy enough, and even stopped at the Old Post Office to see what the wives of the Barnsley supporters were up to. It looked like they were about to get what their husbands' team had just got, so we supped off and left with a smile on our faces.

Our next visit was with kids in tow – and Nige. The Old Post Office had signs that stated "no football coaches", which we thought a little harsh on Don Howe and Terry Venables, and "no football colours" which is fair enough, expect for Nige. Nige had on a Sunderland shirt, socks, and tracksuit – and probably Sunderpants as well. We decided that we'd try a spot of negotiation, and Nige had absolutely no chance of a pint in town. The barman was entirely accepting of our claims that we'd be no bother. Apparently, the signs were there in response to a visit by Millwall on their way to Huddersfield not long before. They had drunk all the spirits, smashed up the bar, broken wind, and tried to nick the bandit. In the words of our new Yorkshire chum "you lot last time drank all our beer, sang a few songs, and were no bother - you're OK for a pint or two." Which is how it should be. We even played there in a friendly to celebrate the opening of their new covered stand, in which we sat next to newly-signed Dean Whitehead's brother. Well, it was either Deano's brother or someone in a Deano mask. Fellow new boy Liam Lawrence was refused entry to the club car park that day, because he didn't have a Barnsley club pass ("look at that blonde ponce" I thought as he roared up in his Audi TT "oops, he's one of us"). As we waited to enter the ground, we were accosted, in the most harmless of manners, it has to be said, by two local youths who were so far out of their collective trees on solvents, a large carrier bag of which they carried with them, that the local Polis just laughed, called them by their names, and warned them as to their future conduct. Oakwell, Barnsley – handy for a pint, handy for a point or three, and the perfect place to give a game to someone you hadn't even registered properly. Step forward Dominic Matteo, brought in to add some guile to our defence. We lost that debacle 4-0. 'Nuff said.

B Is also For Blackpool

Blackpool, eh? I expect most of us could write a book about this place, mainly due to the nature of the town, and the fact that you could call in before or after matches anywhere in the Lancashire area. Does anyone else remember the Sunderland supporter who was discovered with a hacksaw in a back room beneath the tower, trying desperately to "cut the bugger down"? Or being asked by the management not to climb on the tables in the Tower Ballroom, only to spot, minutes later, a member of their bus party sitting astride the moose's head on the wall, leading the singing?

We had a good laugh at Tommer when he jumped onto what he thought was a pile of straw at the bottom of the steps onto the beach. It turned out to be debris on top of a four foot deep puddle, and Tommer had to change into his 1970s disco gear to go to the match. Our most eventful trip came in May 1976, when we assembled a small convoy of cars at Rushyford, and the cream of the youth of Bishop, Shildon, and Aycliffe, dressed in the agreed uniform of the day (granddad shirts, waistcoats, and flat caps) and set off in high spirits.

We arrived ridiculously early, and as the pubs were not yet open, began the day with a plodge and a game of footy on the beach in glorious sunshine. We impressed locals and visitors alike with our silky skills, but I'll bet that none of them would have thought that, a mere six years later, one of our number would be playing in the World Cup Finals. OK, it might only have been for New Zealand, and they might have lost all three games and let in twelve goals in the process, scoring twice – against Scotland – but it was the World Cup Finals. Anyhow, knackered from our exhibition match, we toured the Pleasure Beach and the Funhouse until eleven bells sounded, and the bars were open. We decided to take in some of the local culture, and duly entered a club owned by the boxer, Brian London. We were told by the management that they wouldn't tolerate any "bovver", to which we readily agreed, and we tossed the football behind the bar for them to look after. At 50p for a pint of Double Diamond, it was the least they could do.

The star performer was a professional pie-eater masquerading as an exotic dancer, working a dance-floor the size of a small dining table, surrounded by a dozen slavvering teenagers. It was testament to her skills as a performer that she was heckling the crowd, mostly with gestures involving the waving of a curved little finger in the direction of anyone who made reference to her physical attributes, accompanied by an offer to take the gobby ones outside to see if they knew what to do with it.

Our thirst for culture satisfied, we headed back into the sunlight, and, searching for fellow supporters, eventually spotted a group of fifty or so youths chanting what we thought was "Wearsiders, Wearsiders" at the other side of the promenade near the North Pier. Naturally we ran to join forces, waving our scarves from our belts and wrists as we went. Only when we were amongst them did we hear clearly what they were chanting. "Seasiders, Seasiders." Oh bugger, why does tangerine look so much like red from a distance? Perhaps watching exotic dancers really does make you both blind and deaf. We eventually managed to shake them off with a second, unscheduled, visit to the Pleasure Beach.

The football was a bit of a let down to say the least, although we were heading for certain promotion with this being the penultimate game. Trevor Swinburne was in for Monty, and Mickey Henderson for Tricky Dicky Malone – and young Mick didn't disappoint, seeming to out-Joe Bolton our left back in terms of lifting a few opponents. Moncur and Jacky Ashurst completed the defence which kept the home side out on all but the one vital occasion, while Towers, Ray Train, Gary Rowell – making his fourth appearance and third start - and Billy Hughes made up a midfield that possessed enough attacking power to win the game, but didn't. Neither did the attack of Holden and Pop, and we stumbled to a 1-0 defeat. A typical Sunderland late-season hiccup on the way to the Championship, a typical response to a nice day in the sun. We had arranged to meet up in the pub right next to the bus station after the match, and, as we gathered, it became apparent that it was not the best idea in the world. The pub quickly transformed itself from a happy Blackpool boozer, containing a few tourists, to the Alamo. It was packed with Sunderland boys with the same plan as us, but surrounded by every boot-boy in Blackpool.

We counted up and realised we were a man short. Where was Big Harrier? Our question was answered shortly by the sight of the aforementioned Big Harrier, looking like a red and white Christmas tree, wading through the tangerine hordes towards the sanctuary of the pub, as if they were no more than pensioners on a shopping trip. I should perhaps explain that Harrier did not carry the prefix "big" just for fun. He was, and still is, six foot four, built like something from behind your grandma's house, and played rugby for London Scottish for years. All of which goes some way to explaining his survival of Blackpool Bus Station.

After several abortive escape attempts by the lads, the boys in blue eventually turned up and dispersed the crowd outside. Unfortunately they didn't disperse them very far, and our escape party was soon fragmented by a couple of guerrilla attacks between the pub and the cars. Myself, Dunny, and Chris crept though a series of back streets towards the motors, armed only with a table leg and sock with a brick in it – for self defence only, yer honour – thankfully having to fend off only the one more ambush. Come to think of it, if Dunny hadn't hurled abuse at the bloke with the Blackpool scarf in the doorway of a pub, they wouldn't have thought it necessary to ambush us. The ignorance of youth, I suppose.

Back at the convoy of cars, we managed to assemble all but two of our party, and were about to leave them behind according to the usual Blackpool trip rules – collateral damage, so to speak, and not a bad casualty rate – when a familiar figure came sprinting up the road. He explained how he had just escaped from yet another besieged pub, and that our last man was in the protective custody of the landlord thereof. We quickly formulated a plan. I was driving my mam's Mini Traveller, which, for the benefit of our younger readers, was basically a van with windows, so the idea was as simple as it was surprisingly effective.

I simply drove past the pub with the back doors open and the horn blaring, and on my second pass, our last man burst out of the pub door, through the crowd outside, and in to the back of the Mini. We sped down the road with him hanging onto the back seat, legs trailing behind us, and the Blackpool nutters chasing after in a scene reminiscent of a Keystone Cops comedy. When we got a safe distance from our impromptu pick-up point, I slowed down sufficiently for him to climb aboard and change his pants.

The convoy reassembled as arranged, outside the last pub before the motorway, where we swapped stories of chases and escapes, and got everybody back into the cars they'd arrived in. No serious injuries, nobody nicked by the law, and most importantly no scarves lost. When I got home, mam asked if the car had been OK. I said that it had been fine apart from the back doors coming open as we drove through the streets of Blackpool. Luckily, I had got rid of the table leg and the sock with the brick in it in Barnard Castle. It was as near to the truth as I was prepared to take her, as there was promotion on the horizon and thus the possibility of the car being needed for trips to even more exotic places the following season.

B lackburn (aren't there a lot of teams beginning with "B"? – and they're nearly all in Lancashire and Yorkshire)

I always think of Blackburn's ground in terms of glazed tiles around the turnstiles and meat pies, rather than the three-quarters of a modern ground that is Ewood Park's present incarnation. I preferred the old version, to be honest, but progress is inevitable in today's game. What remains unchanged is the ability of the locals to get a free view of the match from the grassy hillside behind the stand on the right of that usually occupied by the away fans.

One particular trip we took to Blackburn was in the heady days of Jimmy Adamson, who, when he wasn't driving around the pubs of Whitley Bay in his Ford Granada (the football managers' car of choice), was trying his best to sign the entire Burnley team. Could Doug Collins have been done under the Trades Description Act for putting "professional footballer" on his CV? I think so. This was a Christmas fixture, back in the good old days when we used to play games on consecutive days, and we had played Blackpool at home on Boxing Day, the day before. Two goals from a certain Mr G. Rowell ensured the ongoing development of his very own world, to be occupied by Sunderland fans for years to come. At the time, Blackpool had a particularly foolish forward, whose name escapes me, but who was daft enough to cross swords with Joe Bolton. Anyone over the age of forty should remember the incident, or one similar. You know how it went with Birtley's finest - something like this:

1. Joe clatters the forward (nothing unusual there).
2. Forward takes umbrage, and throws punch at Joe. Idiot.
3. A deathly silence descends Roker as the crowd anticipates the inevitable.
4. Forward's face comes into sharp contact with Joe's forehead.
5. Joe sets off for the bath without giving the ref time to get his book out.
6. Two minutes later, forward wakes up.

It makes you wonder – did Joe look at the opposition's teamsheet, spot a worky-ticket winger, and turn the taps on at five to three?

As a result of his dismissal, Joe was not allowed to travel on the team coach the next day, but as a local lad who loved SAFC, he came down on the bus from the Barley Mow anyway, and we spotted him on the terraces at Ewood Park. It being Christmas, I was back in South West Durham for the festivities, and Dowse provided transport for as many as you could squeeze into a purple Cortina Mark 3. It was when we stopped for a pre-match pint at a big pub called the Saxon, near Burnley, that we found out the reason for Joe's exclusion from the team bus. Both the Sunderland and Blackpool teams had stopped there for dinner, and Joe's presence may well have dented the entente cordiale that was evident between the two sets of players. We soon picked out the foolish forward – he was sporting a black eye that stretched from his eyebrow to his top lip, and looking a bit sorry for himself, as you would if you had a face like a panda.

We enjoyed a bit crack with the Sunderland players and staff, as well as Blackpool coach Stan Ternent who had joined us from Carlisle, knacked his knee, and got no closer to playing than the subs bench on a trip to Brighton before going behind the scenes. He reckoned we must have travelled by helicopter to get to Burnley from Bishop in the time we claimed we had. Also full of chat was Bob Hatton of Blackpool, who either mistook us for someone else, or had a bloody good memory – we had spoken to him before or after games on a couple of occasions, but never imagined he would walk up to us and say "alright lads, how are you doing?" and enter into a discussion on the quality of the beer, as if with long-lost friends.

There was also a bus in from Bishop, and one of the lads began berating Mr Adamson about the amount of money he was allegedly earning, and telling him that he should get a round of beers in for the whole bus. Jimmy looked very uncomfortable, as you do when you're a hundred miles from Sunderland and half of Bishop turns up and interrupts your carefully arranged team dinner. However, the tension eased when he surprisingly agreed to this quite moderate request for liquid refreshment. This only went to prove one of three things:

1. We were paying him far too much
2. That he was very generous, or
3. He'd heard about the Aclet Hotel, and went for the sensible option.

Whatever the reason, it showed generosity befitting the season, lightened the mood in the bar, and gave Mr Adamson a better reputation than he deserved in certain parts of Bishop.

The game wasn't much to write home about, but Joe's enforced absence gave a rare chance for Tim Gilbert at left back. Behind him was Barry Siddall, and alongside him at the back were Mickey Henderson – a bit of a radgie at times, so Joe's absence wouldn't be that keenly felt – Jackie Ashurst, and Mick Docherty. Maybe not a defensive line-up that ranks up there with the greatest, or even most memorable in our history, but one that was high on effort and tenacity. The midfield of Kerr, Wonder Wilf Rostron, Arnott, and Greenwood supported Wayne Entwistle and Gary Rowell, but with Greenwood breaking forward and Rowell equally comfortable dropping back to fill in when this happened, we had a fair amount of flexibility in the side. A crowd of over 22,000 is about what we see at Ewood in the 21st century, so not much has changed there. Sanddancer Tim Gilbert had made the bench only once since leaving it to make his debut exactly a year earlier when he replaced Bob Lee in a defeat at Sid James Park, and hadn't got onto the field, so this was his full debut and it was an eventful one. Four months after his nineteenth birthday, he got booked, and fired a low shot from the edge of the box into the net in front of the visiting fans to send us wild with delight. Unfortunately, Blackburn scored as well, and, despite us bringing on Bob Lee to add a bit of height in place of Wayne the punk, it ended as a draw. Conversation as we flew (not literally) back to the land of the Prince Bishops was naturally enough about our promising new left back. Despite being immediately replaced by Mr Bolton for the next game, Tim was back in for the following eight matches. Sadly, Joe's dominance at left back restricted Tim to a total of 43 appearances and three goals before he moved to Cardiff in '81 and Darlington a year later. Even more sadly, he was only 36, and coaching back in Sunderland, when he died.

Thanks to Dowse's helicopter-speed Cortina, we were back in Bishop in plenty of time to carry on the Christmas celebrations and gather our thoughts for our next trip, to yet another B, yet another Lancashire club.

Burnley also starts with B

It was only four days later, on New Year's Eve, that we set off for Burnley. What with it being Christmas and New Year, getting a carful for this was a bit of a problem, as everybody wanted to be certain of a seat in the Cumberland early on, just so they'd not miss out on one come midnight, and we couldn't guarantee what time we'd be back. Tubby had a newish Escort, was happy to show it off, and Stubber was never one to let the prospect of missing out on a seat in the pub spoil a trip to the match, so off we went, just the three of us. Our first New Year's Eve drink was in Accrington, and if ever a town's fortunes mirrored the fortunes of its football team, this was it. I don't know if it has picked up any since the team had life breathed back into it, but back then it wouldn't have looked out of place in a spaghetti western. The whole place looked like it had gone bust in the early sixties. Even the Vauxhall Viva behind us at the traffic lights burst into flames, and we watched the driver frantically beating at the blazing engine with his jacket, instead of following our example and getting the hell away from it. The Rolls Royce (must have been a stranger), behind him, which, as we all know, carried a full fire fighting kit, pulled alongside as if to render assistance, and then zoomed off down the street. Not the spirit of Christmas at all.

Our pint in the town was enlivened by Stubber's usual success on the fruit machine – he managed to get all of the lights on it flashing frantically, but didn't have a clue what to do next. As we stood in a small circle around this impressive, but baffling, 1970s equivalent of a laser disco, the barman leapt over the counter, and pressed another four buttons on the machine. "There you go, lads," he proclaimed proudly, as he stood back to await the fruits of his labours. As we waited for the inevitable torrent of coins, the bandit flashed a slightly different sequence of lights, made some whirring noises, and plopped a solitary ten pence piece into the tray. The barman looked suitably impressed, and went back to work. Stubber collected his winnings, bought two bags of crisps between the three of us, and we left. It just about summed up Accrington – think small and you won't be disappointed.

On to Burnley, which is only a slightly upmarket version of Accrington, and to the football. Turf Moor was a hole in the ground back in the 70s, and the natives were most certainly not of the friendly variety. Once in the ground, we found we were located in the same side as the home fans, from whom we were separated by a worryingly rickety iron fence, New Year Spirit arrived early, in the form of a half bottle of Bell's hitting me in the chest, still with a couple of shots left in it. Cheers, lads, nothing like a shot of the Water of Life to keep out the winter chill and steel the nerves in the face of blatant hostility. The locals continued in this festive vein throughout the first half, spending most of the time throwing bottles and bricks over the fence at us. This fence ran down the middle of the side terraces, and the Polis decided it was sufficient to keep the Burnley fans on the appropriate side, and duly positioned themselves between us and the fence. It kept them on the appropriate side right enough, but it didn't stop them the from pulling the metal posts out of the fence and poking them at us, before launching them into the air above us, reminiscent of a scene from Zulu. Being young and daft, I had decided that a nice big Homburg hat, courtesy of one of Sunderland's finest second-hand shops, was just the fashion statement that the travelling Roker fans should consider at the time, and would look great at away games. A focal point, if you like. It was, and they didn't like. They, of course, being the home fans, who seemed to regard it as something of a target. At least it provided a bit of protection from the lighter of the missiles that rained down on us.

The changes to the team that had won a point at Blackburn earlier in the week were the return of Bolton at the back, meaning no place for the unlucky Gilbert, and of Jeff Clarke alongside Ashurst in front of them, which allowed Docherty to move into midfield. Alongside him were Kerr, Rostron, and Arnott, which meant a rather lightweight attack of Rowell (normal weight) and Greenwood (very light), with Entwistle missing out. Perhaps unsurprisingly, we didn't score, but the return of Big Jeff helped to ensure that they didn't either, and once again we had a Lancashire point to celebrate. To be honest, it was one of those games where the result was way better than the game, and we were much happier with the draw than Burnley were.

Well, we had a New Year party to get back to, so we decided to leg it back to the car as fast as our little legs would carry us. Unfortunately, we had parked facing into a dead end back street, so that a hasty exit was extremely difficult. A quick exit would have been handy, as my distinctive headgear had been noted by the prowling Burnley boys. This was its first and last football outing - it was back to the tried and tested, multi-cultural, flat cap for me.

We listened to Lynyrd Skynrd all the way home (strange what you remember, isn't it?), and flew along the A66 as I lay across the back seat singing "Freebird". Lack of traffic meant that we arrived home in plenty of time for Tubby to park up in Shildon, get down to Bishop, and claim our seats in the Station – the Cumberland was, strangely enough, bereft of empty seats by the time we got there. Ah well, you win some, you lose some, and you draw some. We celebrated the approaching turn of the year by cheering loudly as Stubber kindly ensured our anonymity at future away games by putting a match to my Homburg. Not top of the landlord's list of celebrations, but it drew a decent round of applause from the revellers as midnight approached, and it gave us a laugh.

Brentford

In January 2005, Sunderland were in the throes of yet another questionable season. That's being a bit generous - very generous, actually, as we were on our way to a Premiership record for the second time, and not a record we want to remember. After a month or so of playing well but getting no reward, we had finally put the words luck, good, and Sunderland in the same sentence with a bit of a strawky goal and a deserved victory at The Hawthorns. This gave us the chance to watch Mag Steve Watson deflect the ball into the net on the hour, every hour for a week thanks to Sky Sports, which got our spirits up for the FA Cup third round tie at Brentford. A chance to make our improved luck count for something against a lower league side and a chance to visit a proper old ground. The good luck seemed to be rubbing off on our long-term sick as well, with Kevin Kyle's rehabilitation continuing against Blackburn reserves, when he was every inch the senior pro, and with Stephen Wright bombing about like a madman as McCartney tried his best to get his foot behind his head as he warmed up. We listened nervously for a snapping sound, but it didn't come and George looked as fit as a butcher's dog when he got his run-out. If our injury list was really getting shorter, perhaps there was a cost-saving opportunity for the club with the possible reduction in the size of our team of physios. Just a thought.

The promised Siberian weather not having arrived, it was bright and sunny as we cruised down the M1. We may have seen The Art of War at least once before, but it ticks most of the boxes when it comes to football-journey viewing - violence, action, and an unlikely storyline, even if it is a bit light on the sex side. As we went around the M25 towards Brentford, we got ourselves match-ready by shadow-dealing a few hands of cards, scoffing Ron's lucky FA Cup pie, and mime-drinking a few imaginary pints. We discussed the trial we were giving to the random Irishman who'd retired a couple of years back because of a Kyle-style hip problem, and decided we could probably use him for spares. As we scraped and squeezed the bus around the suburban streets surrounding Griffin Park, we noted that the ground was probably better served for pubs than any other ground in the world. I'd heard that there was a pub on each corner, and that seemed to be true, but there also seemed to be about three more to spare. Brentford – Brentford Nylons; Alan Fluff Freeman used to advertise their horrible nylon bedding – ask yer dad about the nasty little bobbles that formed on them, and the fact that they could give you an electric shock if you moved too fast when lying on them. As there were no longer any shops selling them, we headed down to the High Street, where, on the recommendation of Mr Way Down South, we gave The Beehive a try, and found it 50/50 home and away fans, both in red and white. Our lot were instantly recognizable as the ones shouting for Cheltenham as the dirty Mags took on yet another team in red and white, and we naturally supported anyone who was playing that lot, with the colour of their shirts being a bonus. We left them to their good-natured boisterousness, and moved on to The Magpie and Crown just down the road, only entering because I promised Ron that I'd mention his reservations at entering an establishment with such a name. If anything, it was even busier than the Beehive, the second pint (Grand Union Honey Beer, just for the record) arrived in a Tudor tankard (ask yer dad - it's one of those lumpy things with a handle that rubbish beer like Tartan and Double Diamond used to be served in), and the third in a plastic glass/container. Thankfully, we'd noticed the lack of glass glassware and kept our dirty ones to empty the contents of the plastic efforts into. Little things, I know, but they affect the match day experience, and no-one in their right mind prefers a plastic glass. Perhaps it was an indication of our resignation to our fate, even though I'll always maintain that we're not down until we're down, that I accepted the offer from Mike of the Rutland Branch, who we've met many times in The Lamb and elsewhere, of directions to a good pub in Ipswich for the next season. Shame on me, but I was proved right well before the end of that awful season.

Off to Griffin Park and a welcome step back in time at £12 a ticket to stand, and there we were standing staring into the sunset as the teams appeared. After a game and a bit of football, Kyler was deemed ready to start, when I thought, justifiably as it turned out, that he'd have been better employed chained to the bench for an hour or so and unleashed in a real temper. A defence of Calamity Kelvin Davis, the Collins non-twins of Neill and Danny, Gary Breen, and loanee Justin Hoyte was surely good enough to keep our humble opponents at bay. The front two of Kyle and Jon Stead was surely a clever combination of skill and strength that could overcome our humble opponents, while our midfield of Liam Lawrence, Dean Whitehead, Arca, and Tommy Miller was surely far too much of a mixture of hard work and skill for our humble opponents. One thing we should have learned over the years was that, whenever we thought "surely", we were in for a torrid time. As it was, Neill Collins, in for Steve Caldwell, threw up a hand that didn't even change the path of the ball on only five minutes or so, was booked, and seemed on tenterhooks thereafter. Arca was scarcely seen in the first half, and Brentford looked a lot keener and sharper than us. As had been the case for what seemed like forever, we struggled to cope with pace (DJ Campbell) and brawn (Owusu) in the opponent's forward line, and it took us about forty minutes to put any sort of shape into our play. Whitehead brought a decent save out of their keeper, and we looked to be building up to something when we ran out of time. Then the real fun began. While we'd enjoyed the nostalgic terracing bit, the nostalgic toilets bit was rotten. Two doors, no sort of "in out" organisation, and the question of "why not sort out an entrance/exit strategy" to the three police loitering near one of the doors brought the classic response of "it's not our job". Once we'd plodged through that dark, cramped, and flooded West London version of the Black Hole of Calcutta, and survived, we watched as another nostalgic event took place - the charity blanket to throw coins at. Most missed, someone made a vain attempt to collect them from the pitch, and several dozen coins were still on the playing surface when the second half began - but Sunderland got little change from the pitch or the opposition. The team carried on where they'd left off, and Dean Whitehead played in Jon Stead. As we checked our betting slips, believing that this was to be the moment, Jonboy knocked it wide, then later headed agonisingly past the post. Would the bloke ever score, we thought? Surely the goal had got to come sometime? There we went again – using the "surely" word. We even contrived to give Brentford a couple of decent chances before Campbell burst through, rounded Davis, and we were behind.

We struggled to create anything of quality, but Hoolio, who had gradually got himself into the game, produced one of the worst crosses of his career, and it turned into our second jammy goal in as many games as it drifted over the keeper and in for the equaliser, right in front of us visiting fans. Celebrating from a standing start is so much better than from a seat, and the spilling down the terraces like so many daft teenagers was an absolute joy, arriving, as we did, only a couple of feet from the ruck of celebrating Sunderland players with the little Argentine, fist clenched, popping out of the middle of it. A lovely image and a rare moment of joy that sorry season. As the game wore on, a draw looked about as much as we deserved, and we were right up to the clock when Campbell knocked the ball past Neill Collins, ran into the box, and finished hard and low across Davis. No time to get anything back, the whistle went, Brentford's fans spilled onto the pitch, and the nervous stewards were suddenly backed up with a policeman each. As we vented our displeasure, some asked for the police to remove the Brentford fans from the pitch. "Not our job" was the less than tactful answer. Several fans took out their frustration on the nearest figure of authority, and several stern warnings were given. Brentford had deserved their win, as they were clearly the better team. Martin Allen had assembled a side that worked hard for each other and fights for the collective cause (sound familiar?), which had twice as many shots as us, had a speedy forward with an eye for goal, and a busy midfield. Stead had precious little service, but failed to make anything of the chances he did get, while Kyle's selection in the starting eleven was proved to be a mistake. Plenty of effort, but precious little match practice meant precious little return. Their replacements produced even less, with Andy Gray giving away a free-kick every time he got the ball, and Le Tallec being all French and tarty. I know it's a picky thing, but short sleeves and gloves show a distinct lack of common sense. At the back, Collins (N) and Breen worked hard to contain the Brentford attack - and in the final analysis, they didn't manage it. Collins (D) failed to bring Arca in to the game often enough, and Justin Hoyte (whatever happened to him?) should have known that tackles involve the whole foot and not just the toe end. Dean Whitehead looked knackered towards the end, probably because Tommy Miller had yet another invisible day, forcing his partner into more than his fair share of effort. At least the game was played in a decent spirit, with no petulance or sneakiness - precious little to make us feel happy, but we were determined to get something positive out of the game.

Personally, I could have done with an off-licence stop on the way to the bus, as the afternoon had left me with a craving for about half a bottle of Jameson's. No offy, either allowed or actual, no Jamey's, no chance to drown my sorrows until Bish, and that looked decidedly in the balance when someone chose to run over a rabbit near Doncaster and we were held up for a good while. One film (the name of which I forget, so it must have been a stinker), three episodes of Blackadder, and two of Tony Hancock (ask yer granddad) later, we were back, but not until the obvious text message had arrived – "just the league, then." We did make The Grand before eleven, thankful for small mercies and several pints.
As my text had said - just the League, then.

Bloody hell man... Bolton next

Now that Bolton play at one of the better new grounds – better in the sense that it's a little bit different from most of the flatpack kit jobs that have sprung up over the last fifteen years or so, although it is in a retail park with a motorway nearby – many folks will have forgotten that they used to have a real ground, in the town, next to shops, houses, and pubs. I remember Burnden Park before its last incarnation, when it was a proper ground, without a supermarket in the middle of the away end. Finance, or the lack of it, necessitated the Wanderers doing something to appease the bank manager, but the outcome looked bloody ridiculous after this monstrosity was inserted. OK, so it did give you the chance to buy out of date Easter eggs for dinner on our visit in 1995, when the visitors were housed in the huge open terracing behind the goal – the Supermarket End? – and me and our Ian were subjected to a close up of Brett Angell's close control. Well, if you controlled your bladder with the skill Brett exhibited that day, you'd be standing in a puddle. Two decades earlier, during the 75-76 season, almost 100,000 people watched the two games between SAFC and Bolton, and we were in the crowd at Burnden for the away game. They seem to have lost the interest for football since those heady days.

As always seems the case in these tales, it was December 27th, and we travelled in style to this one – Lino borrowed the Simca 1100 van from work. If you've never seen one of these, you're not alone – they weren't a very popular vehicle, the details of which have probably been expunged from all Ladybird Books of Cars, Observers' Book of Cars, and Haynes manuals. It was a horrible, vicious, little thing, but we couldn't really say so at the time, for fear of offending the driver and not getting a lift. This van had two front seats, and a coarse mesh between them and the cargo bay where most of us sat. Lino's driving at the time can probably be best described as adventurous, and it often resulted in us in the back making like spacemen in an anti-gravity chamber. We were tossed about at every corner, and frequently came out of the van with the imprint of the coarse mesh stamped on our faces, making us look like waffles. We used to exact revenge by scrawling obscenities on the interior of the van, in the hope that he would get into trouble at work.

Anyhow, Lino offered to drive us to Bolton. In fact, he offered to drive most of South West Durham to Bolton, but we didn't complain, as he had a claim to fame. His granddad, Harold Archer Brown, had played centre forward for Sunderland in the 1920s, he said. Subsequent checking of records revealed that the ancestor in question signed from his hometown club Shildon – which we from Bishop refused to hold against him, we were bigger than that - at the end of 1921, played six times, and scored on his debut as we beat Man Utd at Roker. Sadly, he didn't trouble the scorekeepers in his next five games, none of which we won, and by the end of February 1922 was away – to the football hotspots of Leadgate, Chilton, Shildon, and QPR. Six games for a transfer fee of £650 was a pretty big investment back then, so we reckoned that Lino should pay the Sunderland fans back by providing lifts whenever he could. His grandson and I probably spent more time on the Roker Park turf celebrating goals than Harry did playing football, but a red and white granddad is still a claim to fame.

There were no seats in the back of this van, but we were packed so tight it didn't really matter. Big Harrier got the front seat, as usual, and for obvious reasons, with the crate of beer beneath his legs, passing bottles over or under the mesh whenever thirst got the better of those in cattle class, which was quite often. I don't know whether there were three, four, of five of us in the back that day, but, when we got to Tebay, the van stopped. Ah, time for a run-off, as Shakespeare would have said – but we were wrong. Lino had decided to play the Good Samaritan, and pick up two hitch hikers, complete with mountaineering–sized rucksacks. Oh joy!

We made the rest of the journey pass quickly by singing, drinking, sitting on top of each other, drawing on the walls, and generally frightening the poop out of our two new friends. We also found that we could open the tailgate from inside by pulling on a wire, but the expressions on the faces of the motorists following down the M6 persuaded us that this was not the best idea in the world. That and the very real possibility of falling out and spilling our beer, so we went back to graffiti and drink.

As mentioned earlier, there was a big, big crowd – forty-odd thousand, to be less than precise –and we only just made the kick-off, high up at the back of the open end, pre-supermarket. These were two of the division's big guns, and this was officially going to be a big match. Gary Rowell, a debutant from the bench as we beat Oxford at home a fortnight earlier, was on the bench again, with the remnants of the Boys of '73 starting the game. Monty, SuperDick Malone, Joe Bolton, Jeff Clarke and Jackie Ashurst at the back, and a midfield of…well, a strange midfield. Kerr and Towers, fair enough, we knew all about those two, and Tom Finney of Northern Ireland, whose best midfield berth I could never work out, but he could play wide, he could play an attacking central role, and, most frequently, he could warm the bench. He was named as substitute 26 times but only actually got on the field on 21 occasions. Today he was in central midfield, but, supposedly to add some bite, making up the quartet was Mickey Henderson. If you've any memory at all of Mickey, it will be of a no-nonsense (rough as bull's lugs, hard as nails, helping to fashion a mould in which John Kay would be forged – you get the picture) full-back and not as a midfielder. But there he was, and he was there to back up Pop Robson and Mel "Rules the Skies" Holden.

The match, for once in the "big match" circumstances, actually lived up to expectations, even if the result was all wrong from our point of view. It looked like it was going our way when ex-Man U defender Tony Dunne put away a Bobby Kerr cross for a superb OG, and we were already planning our post-match celebrations back in Bishop, but we showed true SAFC generosity and let them score twice to send us home pointless. Never mind, it was one of only ten games we lost all season – all away from home, so there's more typical Sunderland behaviour for you – as we dropped only two points at Roker and took the Championship of the then Second Division, now Championship. We endured a dry trip home on this occasion, as we were typically rubbish at pacing ourselves and saving a bottle or two for the return journey, and being of that certain age when we had no money left for an off-licence stop. We watched in surprise as hitchikers hid behind bushes and ditches as we passed – word sharp gets around, eh? – and Lino's van got decorated some more. Some of it was pretty obscene, to be honest, but he never let on whether or not he got into trouble at work or not, but, knowing him, he'll have talked his way out of it. He had more neck than a giraffe when it came to excuses.

is not for Bradford (as we're still onto B)

I think of Bradford for two main reasons. Firstly, it is always really cramped even since the redevelopment that followed the awful events of 1985, and secondly, Bradford has been a happy hunting ground for me – I've been there many times, and we've won a good proportion of those games. Four times I've seen us score four goals there (with only one in return in those games, incidentally). Add to that the fact that it's just down the road (in Sunderland terms) and Stubber lives there, so I get the chance to stay over and discuss the finer points of our victories in the company of some dead cheap Sam Smith's beer. I remember my first victory being courtesy of a bit of magic from Kieron (where's me burger?) Brady. Denis Smith had been quoted in the press that week as saying that Brady was extremely talented, but had to realise that he couldn't expect to beat four men and score in the Football League. Kieron chose the Bradford game to beat at least seven men and score in front of the visiting fans. That was the start of a run of lovely wins.

However, despite the undoubted drama of the visit when Quinny elevated himself to the status of everlasting hero by scoring the only goal of the game, then replacing the injured Sorensen in goal and keeping a clean sheet to win us the game – what he was to do in the future should have come as no surprise to us after that - it is the previous visit which I remember most fondly. Stubber and I share the same birthday, and it happens to be September 5th, so an obvious birthday treat in 1997 would be an away victory on that date. Boy, did we get a present to remember! We had front row seats above Lionel, and kept the noise at top level rattling the advertisement hoardings for ninety minutes, as you do when you reach the landmark age of forty one. Good old Lionel kept a clean sheet, which wasn't that difficult when the opposition had about as much bite as Barbara Cartland with her teeth out. Makin, Scott, Ord, and Melville kept the hapless homesters at bay, while Lee Clark (boo hiss), Johnston, Bally, and Mickey Gray fed the bullets to Superkev and the Martin Smith. For all the undoubted magic in the boots of the front two, it was Gray, Johnston, and Clark who added to SKP's goal, and I've seen few away games where players were on the verge of laughter. 4-0 flattered Bradford, to be honest, and was the perfect excuse for a night out on the town. After the match, Pos took the kids home to Bishop (as he didn't have a pass-out from she-who-must-be-obeyed), allowing Stubber and me to change our shirts and hit the Emmott Arms in Yeadon, near the airport, and handily just across the field from his house. If you've ever been on a night out around Bradford, you'll know a couple of things: firstly, you don't see too many Bradford supporters in the pubs away from the city centre, and secondly, Sunderland colours are not the most popular in the Leeds area. Apparently, their memories of 1973 are just as vivid as ours, but entirely opposite.

For the second of the above reasons, it is advisable to be subtle in your display of red and white in the pubs, despite the fact that there are a surprisingly large number of Sunderland regulars around Yeadon. At Stubber's promotion party the day after Barnsley in 1999, for instance, I was talking to a South Shields exile by the name of Bees whose scarf had been on Top Of The Pops in 1973. Apparently this was because the guitarist in the group "Geordie" was a Mackem, and had borrowed the scarf to show his true colours. A little bit of rock'n'roll trivia for you.

So, we ordered a double round of the famously cheap Sam's, sat down amongst the Leeds fans to wistfully celebrate the passing of yet another year, and gleefully relived the exhilaration of the match. We had sensibly chosen to display our Wearside allegiance by means of subtle shirts bearing the club crest. We'd managed half an hour or so of quiet giggling, optimistically planning how to celebrate promotion the following May, and noisily whacking back the Sam's when we became aware of a pair of eyes staring at us. The guy looked quite sane and sensible, in his late forties, but fit looking. He saw us glance up at him, and moved across, pint in hand. We braced ourselves to talk our way out of whatever was imminent, and he joined us at our table, "Excuse me lads, but I couldn't help noticing your accents. Are you Sunderland Supporters?" "Yes," we replied "Oh good," he said, "I used to play for the youth team a while ago." "A bloody long while," we thought, and entered into a lengthy and fascinating conversation about life as an apprentice at SAFC in the mid to late Sixties. This bloke turned out to have gone to school with Colin Suggett, and remained close friends with him to that day. Our new pal had joined Sunderland at the same time as Suggett and Todd, but had sustained what was, in those days, a career ending leg injury. Modern surgical techniques would probably have ensured his football future, but he decided to go into teaching, and went to a Physical Education college near Bradford. He'd been nearby ever since. The people you meet, eh? We forgot to ask his name, so that we could look him up in the reference books, but we were on our birthday night out, and didn't want to be too anorakish. (Real word? Who cares!)

It made our night, really – a 4-0 win away from home on our birthday, and meeting someone who had turned out in the red and white. We continued our celebrations at Stubber's house in true Bradford fashion – "let's all have a curry" we had sung at the match, so we ordered in a great big hot one with all the trimmings, and washed it down with lashings of Mr Boddington's foamy canned stuff. Happy birthday indeed.

B is for Bristol (City)

It's a long way away, so a trip to Bristol took quite a bit of planning. Well, it did when I had no money to spend back in the summer of '75 – no, actually, I was earning a crust selling ice cream and the truth is that I was simply too tight to spend money when I didn't have to. Some things never change.

This was to be part of my first ever grand tour of away games – a double header involving Bristol on a Tuesday night, and sleeping rough somewhere between there and Oxford, the venue of our next away game the following Saturday. Oh, to be an eighteen year old optimistic hitchhiker again. The season had started well, with a one match unbeaten run courtesy of a 2-1 defeat of Chelsea at Roker. My folks were visiting friends in Newport, so I travelled down with them on the Monday, spent the night on an armchair in South Wales, and took the train to Bristol on Tuesday afternoon.

It was a pretty small turnout by Sunderland standards – there seemed to be only about 150 of us, standing packed together in the middle of the away terraces, singing our heads off – for a while. The game was an absolute disaster, despite Bob Stokoe making only one change to the side that had triumphed over Chelsea, and it looked like a positive one with Mel Holden moving from the bench in place of Tommy Gibb, who took up the number 12 shirt. Aye, just the one sub back in the good old days. Trevor Swinburne continued in goal, and Jackie Ashurst continued at right back, with Joe Bolton, Jeff Clarke, and new skipper Moncur completing the defence. Dennis Longhorn, Bobby Kerr, and Ian Porterfield were the midfield, and perhaps that's where Bob got it wrong as it left us light in the middle, with Pop, Mel, and Vic Halom up front. Poor Trevor Swinburne was horribly exposed by a defence that played like they'd never met, let along played a solid game only a few days before. Wacky Jacky Ashurst was the chief organiser of this disorganisation, as he was no right-back. Now,

Jacky was a better than decent centre-half who gave sterling services to the Lads before a long career at Blackpool, Carlisle, Leeds, and Doncaster before winding down at Bridlington, Rochdale, and Frickley, but he was to right-backs what Tom Ritchie was to goal poachers. In short, he could manage it on the odd occasion, but nowhere near often enough to be described as one. Poor Jacky got skinned every time City came forward, and, right in front of the visiting fans, we were dead and buried after twenty minutes.

Our unhappy band tried to keep up their spirits by singing, but it didn't work. Two down at the break, at least the third goal was at the other end of the ground, so we didn't see it in such vivid detail. Even Tommy Gibb, on for Porterfield, couldn't work his magic or anything else. By the end of the match, plan A, the sleeping somewhere on the way to Oxford plan, had been abandoned. Some lads from Trimdon were going camping in Cornwall for a few days, then going back up to Oxford on the Saturday morning, and they invited me along. Tents sounded better than sleeping rough, so I agreed, despite having only a few quid in my pocket and nothing to wear other than what I stood up in. As soon as the whistle went, we set off towards the cars, which were cleverly parked behind the home end. As we passed the open gates of their end, words were exchanged. I don't remember exactly what was said, but it included the words mangle-wurzel, sheep, and sex. Suffice to say that it had a similar effect to the Pope walking into Ibrox, and our little band of prospective campers was quickly fragmented by a veritable cavalry charge of foul-tempered Bristolians. I don't know what they were so upset about – they'd just won 3-0. Perhaps they were stung by our comments being a little close to the truth. Whatever it was, it signalled the end of plan B.

So it was that I found myself, for the first time, in the company of the blonde lad from Huddersfield who used to turn up wherever Sunderland were playing in the seventies. He had no connection with the club, or the area, but followed us through thick and thin. I can't remember what his name was, but I came across him many times over the next few years. I hope he's still out there somewhere, with his Sunderland scarf tied to his wrist. On this occasion, we got to know each other while running round the streets near Ashton Gate, trying to avoid a good kicking. Friendship forged in adversity, I guess. Our first joint decision was to hide from the trouble by pretending to use a telephone box. Based on the experience of hindsight, I will offer this advice to readers: if you are considering hiding from someone in a phone box (assuming you can find one these days), remember that they possess two important features. Firstly, they have full-length windows on three sides, so everyone has a clear view of the contents. Secondly, the door opens outwards, so there is no easy way of keeping it shut from the inside.

Despite these obvious deficiencies in our chosen place of refuge, we managed to keep a particularly vicious-looking skinhead out of the box for what seemed like ages before a police dog and handler persuaded him that he probably had better things to do. We decided that the safest place to be was back inside the ground, so we snuck back in, and climbed into the directors' box. After twenty minutes or so, we decided that it should be safe to leave, as the ground was completely empty. Unfortunately, all of the gates were locked, so the only way to get out was down the players' tunnel. As we passed the changing rooms, we exchanged pleasantries with a couple of the Bristol City players, and then the referee emerged from his room, shook our hands, and thanked us for not resorting to kicking too many City players despite the frustration of our performance. This confirmed our suspicions about the visual capacity of referees, as we looked as much like professional footballers as Anne Widdicome and were dressed exactly like two daft teeneagers at a football match in 1975.

I persuaded my new pal to join me in plan C, which was in fact a reversion to plan A, and we duly set off for the motorway to begin hitching to Oxford. Unfortunately, my days as a geography student were a month away from beginning, and thus my knowledge of the area was poor, and we had no idea of where the motorway was. We managed to find our way to Temple Meads station after nicking a bag of chips from a short-sighted chip shop owner, where we joined forces with another half dozen Sunderland vagrants also with no visible means of getting home, including the famous Sammy. You know Sammy, he was, and still is a legend, having, amongst a horde of other things, painted his dog red and white two years earlier for the FA Cup Final. Sammy's plan that night (let's call it plan X) was to pinch a lift on the mail train and jump off when he thought he was as near to Sunderland as the train got. "What's your plan, young'un?" he asked me, so I explained our intention of hitching to Oxford and roughing it for a couple of days. "You're madder than me" he replied. Now, to an eighteen year old Fulwell Ender, at that particular point in time, this comment was the equivalent of an Oscar, or a knighthood, and I was so happy that another half dozen Sunderland fans were there to hear it. Sammy spent an hour or so playing against type and lifting young ladies' luggage into their taxis, and asking them if anyone had ever told them they were beautiful.

We decided against plan X, as it was strictly illegal, and set off for the M5, ending up at the end of the A38(M) courtesy of a kind-hearted taxi driver who gave the pair of us a free ride there. It was somewhere near Eastville, and four or five of us wasted an hour or so trying ineffectively to thumb a lift until the law arrived. Apparently, some woman in one of the nearby houses had phoned to say that we'd been rampaging through their gardens. Fortunately, the Polis was a decent sort, and maybe the woman in question was a well-known whinger, and he realised we weren't causing any bother. He recommended that we got some kip in a nearby park shelter before resuming our travels at first light. We spent a very cold night – wasn't this August in the South West? – and when I awoke, the others had gone. I made my way back to the roundabout, stuck out my thumb, and resigned myself to a long wait. For once, I was wrong, and within a few minutes, a great big old Ford Zodiac stopped.

"Oxford?" I enquired.

"Arr," came the reply from the driver, and I climbed aboard.

"At the match last night?" he questioned.

"Aye," I replied.

"You useless buggers, you could have won. We're Rovers"

They were on their way to their match that night at Norwich, and were naturally passing through Oxford. Quickly counting my money, I realised that without resorting to crime, I couldn't survive the next few days, so I formulated plan D – or was it C, as the original C hadn't actually been used at all – which was to get to the A1 and thumb it home. This was the best plan so far, as it actually worked, and I got a quick lift on the A1 from a Dutch lorry heading for Tyneside. The driver agreed to drop me at the A68 junction for good old Bishop, and things got even better when he let me root though his collection of Led Zep and Focus tapes and play whichever I fancied. We chatted about music, Dutch football's impressive showing in the previous year's World Cup, and the world in general, as I relaxed and he smoked his pipe. It was only after about an hour or so, when I began to feel decidedly light-headed, that I realised it wasn't St Bruno in his billowing pipe. There I was, hurtling up the A1 in front of several tons of choice Dutch tomatoes, and the driver was as light as a ragman's balloon. Would I survive the journey, or would I end up as part of a giant salad on a roundabout somewhere near Newark? I sat back and inhaled deeply – if you can't beat 'em, join 'em, and it helped to pass the time, making it seem as if it were us that were stationary and the fields were flying south at a ridiculous speed. After what turned out to be quite an enjoyable trip in more ways than one, I landed at Burtree roundabout and hitched a lift back to Bishop with a bloke who couldn't work out why I was grinning so much when I had suffered so badly at the hands of my team the previous evening.

Luckily, my folks were not due back from Wales until Sunday, so I was able to get my head in gear (or should that have been out of gear?) and prepare a git big fry-up. I planned a couple of early nights – Oxford was only a couple of days away, and my hitching thumb needed its beauty sleep before the second stage of plan D.

B is for Bristol (Rovers this time)

Do you remember Persil tickets? If you saved up enough vouchers from the top of the Persil boxes, you could get two train tickets for the price of one. A fine marketing ploy by the manufacturers and one which ensured the cleanliness of all travelling football fans at the time. One of the many times we took advantage of this offer was to travel to Bristol Rovers in April '80.

Sensible as ever, we arrived early lunchtime and I deposited an eight-pack of Maxim in a left luggage locker at Temple Meads – this would ensure no dehydration on the homeward journey, and it was (as it is today) a sight cheaper than buying drink on the train. Cocktails were taken in the city centre as we revelled in the culture of the cosmopolitan South-West, and then the local constabulary marched the Red and White Army en masse to Eastville. This stroll took us through the St Paul's district, which was soon to gain notoriety thanks to what were described at the time as riots or civil disobedience. I think we'd call them war these days. Let's just say it was building up nicely towards them on the occasion of our visit – you could feel tension and unrest in the air. Anyhow, our procession was viewed by the locals as the equivalent of marching down the Scotswood Road wearing a Sunderland top. Muscle-bound monsters armed with baseball bats lined our route, and hurled obscenities at our every step. Mind you, their husbands looked pretty rough as well. My nervous bowel just about held out until we reached the sanctuary that was Eastville – a right tip, but a welcome sight nevertheless.

That particular part of the South West has never been a happy hunting ground for us, as we've won just the one league game and the one League Cup game. Mind, they've never won at our place either, so that just about evens things up.

Anyway, we were cruising nicely towards a table-topping finish to the season, but it being Sunderland, we were well aware that slip-ups were always waiting around every corner. Just under ten thousand were crammed into what was left of the crumbling Eastville, and those in our end (and Wearsiders scattered around the rest of the ground, as usual) were up for a win to keep promotion on track. Whitworth, Hinnigan, Hindmarch, and Jeff Clarke had the job of protecting Turner, while Mick Buckley, Arnott, Barry Dunn, and Stan Cummins were there to provide for Alan Brown and Pop Robson up front. In all honesty, the game provided far less entertainment and much less tension than the walk from the station, and the terraces were a sea of gloom when we went in at the break 2-1 down. A quick inspirational rallying speech from the most eloquent of us set away a feeling of optimism that spread across the away end, and we shouted the Lads on to snatch a draw from the jaws of defeat. Champion. Goals from Barry Dunn and Pop Robson had secured another vital point on the road to eventual promotion from second place, with a home win over Watford, a draw at Cardiff, and that 2-0 win over West Ham being enough. The Dunn goal was a bit special, not in terms of quality (not that it was a bad one), but in terms of rarity, being one of only two he scored for us in his 25 appearances – both away from home, both in draws. We had a soft spot for the lad, as he'd done Northern League time with Tow Law, Bishop, and Blue Star, from whom we signed him. He might have since beaten me at pool, but I refuse to hold that against him because he still follows the Lads. After the match, as we waited the customary fifteen minutes (specifically designed to allow the local thugs to set their ambushes in the surrounding streets) in the away end, the police made the announcement I was dreading. The train home would be making an unscheduled stop at a nearby halt to pick us up, meaning that we did not have to walk all the way back to the city centre. They probably thought that they were doing us a favour, and you have to admit it was a rare attack of common sense on their behalf. But from our point of view, it was nothing less than blind panic. I explained to a policeman that I had some personal items – not precious, but of enormous sentimental value to myself – secured in a left luggage locker at Temple Meads. I held the vain hope that he might agree to an armoured convoy taking our party back through St Paul's to retrieve them, but his answer was what I expected rather than what I hoped for.

"Tough" he said, and with that, all hopes of a night on the Maxim evaporated into the evening air. No "lamp oil" for me. It was only eight cans of Maxim, but just think what they'll be worth now – in their original Vaux cans, a veritable collector's item. I hope some bright spark at Temple Meads had the sense to open the locker when I'd not been to claim my belongings after the prescribed time, and enjoyed a little bit of Wearside at their summer barbecue in the South West.

Luckily, one of our party was of a generous disposition that day, as he must have backed our goalscorer, or found a pound note (remember them?), and let me share his beer – probably to stop me crying. We were lucky, in that the train stopped at Birmingham, allowing us to replenish our stock of liquid refreshment. We performed the usual post-match train home antics of drinking and singing, until we had to change at York. This gave the best laugh of the day, as one of our party decided to ignore the advice of the station staff, and try to board the train that was just leaving, instead of waiting half an hour for the next one. The train of his choice was already moving down the platform when our hero decided that he would get aboard, despite all of the doors being shut. He had spied an open window, and he was going to go for it, whatever we said. Now, let's not name this person, but he knows who he is. Let's also say that he is of the big-boned variety of football supporter, and that he propelled himself through the air with surprising grace, immediately getting a good proportion of his person through the window at the first attempt. Using his unique upper body shape and weight as a counterbalance, he teased his bottom half through the protesting opening, despite catching various items of clothing on the frame.

My everlasting vision is of a pair of flailing legs protruding from the train now departing platform one, revealing a steadily increasing amount of arse as his belt snagged on the window frame, and his body slithered into the carriage with a plop that could be heard back in Bristol.

C is for Cardiff

ardiff, by nature of the fact that it's in another country, is a long way away – far enough to completely bugger up your Friday night. Do you go out early and come back early, go out late and stay out all night, or just stay in? Back in December 2004, and being of the sensible sort, I stayed in, surprised our Gaz by getting up at 4:30, just after he'd got in, and cooking a full English breakfast - obviously bypassing the idiot button on the cooker that prevents anyone from doing fry-up at stupid o'clock. You might expect at least a few hours at the beginning of a trip starting at such an ungodly hour to offer the chance of a bit of a snooze, but no. It was not to be.

05:30 George: "I saw Jools Holland the other night, he was great."
05:31 Ben: "I saw Jools Holland the other night, he was crap."

This was the cue for half an hour of what I'll call heavy debating, and you might call argument, which quickly encompassed hunting, the House of Lords, sherbet fountains and the difficulty in finding them in anything but specialist sweet shops in certain parts of County Durham, and Wendy Richards' new hairdo. This sort of discussion is all very well, but before six on a Saturday is simply unacceptable. A live camera link, and it would have been perfect BBC2 overnight fodder; "Welcome to our latest social arts discussion forum, Five Eejits Argue Earnestly About Bugger-All." We thought that would be a better format for the previous evening's "Fighting Talk" programme on BBC2, on which Steve Cram had defended Glenn Hoddle's appointment as Wolves manager because "Hoddle's a great bloke because he brought Gullit into the English game, and Gullit dropped Shearer, and we all know what happened in the rain." He won the evening's debate and cleverly managed to refer to Shepherd's "dogs" comment. It's nice when someone in the public eye manages to show his support for the Lads, and have a pop at our neighbours at the same time. Top lad.

By the time we'd got ourselves properly awake, it was 10:45, we'd made good time, and we were in Llantiily Breffni. That's Usk in English, and luckily we hadn't had to endure a journey like that of a few years previously when the condition of a certain person's innards required the consumption of half a litre of Pepso Bismol after that certain person had broken the "no solids" rule on the bus, and thus had to make the walk of shame to the organiser to make his apologies. When we'd got to the town, and the certain person had taken advantage of the first pub toilet available for a bit of a sit down, we'd persuaded the local bobby on the beat to confront the perpetrator with a complaint from the motorway services that had, only the week before, won Toilets of the Year. The look on his face when accused of ruining their chances for the foreseeable future was priceless, and also proves that there are lawmen out there who enjoy a laugh as much as we do. Well, maybe not quite as much, but you get the general idea.

As age brings with it a bit of experience, and the sense to actually plan ahead, we'd spent a good bit of the journey poring over a copy of next year's Good Beer Guide. With age also comes an increased fussiness about what we drink before games, unlike in our teens, when any old slops would do. Ron refused point-blank to even consider the Conservative Club as an option, despite if offering the cheapest beer in town. We nipped round the back streets to the Kings Arms, where the door was open, so we popped in to check what time it opened. The landlord, who was in the middle of cleaning out one of the biggest open fires we'd ever seen, told us it would be in about half an hour, but seeing as we were in, he might as well sell us a pint apiece while we waited. That's the kind of landlord that was all too rare, and thus really appreciated, in those far-off days when you needed special permission to open the bar before eleven. We settled round the huge fire, warmed our toes, and enjoyed swapping opinions with the locals, one of whom actually supported the day's opponents. Canny enough lad, but we stopped short of offering him a lift to the game. Having exhausted the options there, which included the Landlord giving us a free try of some toffee-based nonsense called Dooley's (I believe it's made from recycled Cadbury's Crème Eggs and surgical spirit) we headed for the Black Horse with some trepidation. On our precious visit, the landlord had made it known in no uncertain terms that visiting football fans were not the sort of custom his hostelry encouraged or even served. Thankfully, they'd had a change of heart, as we soon discovered on entering. Most of the rest of our bus party had filled the back room, and were indulging in raucous conversation, card games, and even a spot of singing. In short, they were having a bloody good time, so we thought it would be rude not to join in. There was still one hostelry on our list to visit on the way back to the bus, the Nags Head. Actually, it wasn't on the way back to the bus at all, but we'd been before and thought it worth a repeat visit. It had a line on the wall marking where the river Usk had reached when in a particularly bad temper and bursting its banks, but the only water on show was the unique, and really naff, miniature ornamental fountain on the end of the bar. Great beer, despite some of them having Welsh names and being therefore beyond our powers of pronunciation, and more great banter with the locals and staff. Basically, Usk was as friendly as it could have been, and I like to think that the place looks forward to Sunderland's next game in South Wales as an opportunity to welcome us, the fans, to town.

Cardiff, on the other hand, is not noted for welcoming visiting supporters with anything other than open hostility, as well as not being noted for fresh air and fun. Our previous visit had seen us lose – no, we were hammered – 4-0 and had Jocky Bjorklund sent off in a game of abject capitulation. We were also subject to a fair amount of attempted violence by the home fans during the game, then kept back for a good fifteen minutes with the toilets shut. As usually happened on occasions like that, it wasn't long before someone shouted "just like the bloody miners' strike" and an already tense atmosphere turned distinctly ugly. Once outside, there was no attempt to keep the home fans, who were supposed to have dispersed while we were locked in but had clearly decided to ignore this rule, away from our route back to the coaches, and there one or two spots of what we used to call aggro. I believe it is now called interaction, and is frowned upon at all times.

Anyway, that's what we suspected would happen again, so we were understandably on edge when we got off the bus. A decent arrival time in the land of sheep allowed me to question the local Polis as to whether we would be kept in after the game again. He couldn't have been any more friendly, or any less informative, as his reply of "nothing to do with me, boyo, I was off last season". As it was early, and we'd already broken our New Season Resolution not to drink the overpriced fizz that they serve in football grounds, we headed for the bar, reasoning that it was the part of our end furthest away from the more boisterous Cardiff fans, and we were therefore reducing the possibility of "interaction" with them. The lass behind the bar was worth the ticket money on her own, as she showed complete contempt for the rule that football ground bar staff should be, at every available opportunity, sullen, inefficient, and bereft of any sort of humour. On the terraces, the home fans sang that they didn't like us – mind you, I suspect that they don't like anybody English, or anybody from anywhere else in Wales – so we sang dreadfully racist stuff about sheep and Max Boyce, and we played them off the park. It was in some way refreshing to be stood next to a net running from the back of the stand to the front, the purpose of which was to catch missiles thrown by the home fans (acceptable, apparently), while the stewards, bless them, fell about laughing at our songs and attempts at dancing.

It was also, in 2004, a welcome novelty to stand at a football match, with the seats in front of us in a style that is apparently known as Retro-Welsh.

Unlike the previous season, when we'd been as bad as bad could be, that day we were unstoppable. The previous encounter had been in the Nationwide Football League Division One as we had an off-day on our way to defeat in the Play-Off semi-finals, this one was in the Coca Cola Championship as we battered our way to the Championship. There might only have been ten months between the games, and Mick Mac was in charge for both of them, but they were light years apart in terms of performance and spirit. It was the sixth of our thirteen away wins that season, and came courtesy of two goals, from Lawrence and Whitehead, down at the other end of the pitch that looked quite decent. With Thomas Myhre, forever known as Tommy Two thanks to the early part of his stay being as Thomas Sorensen's deputy, in goal, and Stephen Wright the full-back partner for George McCartney, Mick Mac had restored what we referred to as the Breen-Caldwell axis, and the defence were rock-solid all afternoon. Carl Robinson, Arca, Liam Lawrence and Dean Whitehead ran the midfield, while Chris Brown and Stephen Elliott ran the home defence ragged. We even had ready-made front-two replacements in Marcus Stewart and Michael Bridges (cool as fridges) to run the game down, and Mark Lynch to bolster the defence –something that we came to regard as a novelty as far as he was concerned. Winning away from home is always nice – how could it not be? – but winning that far away from home has something a bit special about it. While never the prettiest game in the world, it was a really professional job, and it was only a shame that the goals were down the far end where we couldn't appreciate them fully, as both looked good from where we were, but, when seen on TV, were absolute buck-snorter super duper efforts. Without Earnshaw, working that weekend on a cruise ship as a Sammy Davis Junior lookalike (after falling asleep with his head in the fire), Cardiff were over reliant on enthusiasm rather than skill, and we were clearly the better side. They worked hard, but lacked any real quality.

Just like in the seventies when I'd started this away-match travelling nonsense, it was a long coach trip home on which to celebrate the day's victory. Unlike the seventies, there were motorways virtually all the way back, the bus must have moved a lot quicker, and it didn't have to factor in bladder-relief stops every couple of hours. All of which meant that the bus driver was the man of the match, as he got us back home in time for a couple of celebratory shandies in Bishop. OK, so pub opening hours in 2004 allowed opening until midnight and beyond for no other reason than that folks might want to stay out late, but they do allow the chance for yet another rundown of the day's win.

C harlton Athletic

Charlton just qualifies as a London game – it is geographically in the capital, but has an atmosphere completely differently to any other London club apart from Wimbledon, before their less than sad demise when they played at Selhurst, which had whatever atmosphere the away fans chose to take with them. It is very much a family club nowadays and a good place for a day out, if you can stand another train journey from King's Cross.

We did the usual ICPP trip for the game in the 1994/95 season, keeping up our civilised appearance on the way down by staying off the drink on the train. They're the rules, and we always stick to them apart from when extenuating circumstances prevail – such as when champagne and orange juice are provided, meaning Bucks Fizz for breakfast, or when Gin and Dandelion and Burdock are on the menu – it's a long story, but it does happen from time to time. As we do on such occasions, we met up with Steve and Tony from Chester-le-Street as arranged, and dined at Del's before moving on to the Lamb. Having drunk enough beer to pay for the landlord's holiday, we persuaded him to order us a couple of taxis for the next leg of our journey to the station, and they duly arrived – a Sierra and a Sweeny-style Granada, giving us in the second car the chance to utter the immortal phrase "follow that cab!" So we did.

On the train to Charlton, having stuck our miniature Sunderland scarf on the window (as you do with your car back window), we noticed a couple of youths pointing and sniggering at us, apparently because of the way we spoke. They were duly summoned over to our seat, given a copy of "Viz", open at the Biffa Bacon page, and told in no uncertain terms to read, learn, and inwardly digest. Their attempts to translate Biffa into Cockney were hilarious, and kept us amused until we arrived at Charlton, where we met the next members of our party in the pub nearest the ground. This doesn't sound like a very precise method of making a rendezvous, but before the advent of the mobile phone, it is one that served football supporters well enough for over a century. It works for every ground in the country, and you can always find somebody that you know.

The barman made my day by only charging me for three pints instead of the five he served me, which is a considerable discount at London prices, and then we were approached by a young man selling Charlton scratchcards. He was a little dubious about asking us to buy them, but, as the pub was absolutely chocka with Sunderland fans, he had little choice. Years before, several of our number had made a few bob flogging Roker Bingo tickets, and ever since I'd sold a ten pound winner, I've felt sort of obliged to have a go on that sort of thing when offered. Unfortunately for him, someone had given him a pile of cards that contained at least 74% winners, and every two minutes there was a cry of "I've won – where's me fiver?" The poor lad was virtually in tears when he managed to escape at quarter to three, with less money than he'd come in with. We, on the other hand, came out of the pub as merry as you like and with considerably more cash than we'd gone in with.

Having collected the final members of our group at the turnstiles, we endured one of the worst games inflicted on us by Mr Buxton, and God knows there were plenty of candidates for that dubious honour. We had Chamberlain in goal, Dariusz and Scotty at full back, and Dickie Ord alongside Benno in the centre. That wasn't really a bad defence - in fact, it was a pretty good defence - but it was further up the field where our problems lay. On paper, Derek Ferguson was a fine player, a precise playmaker, and an intelligent user of the ball. The problem with his time at Sunderland was that we played on grass. OK, it's an old one, but it could have been written specifically about Ferguson, as it simply didn't work for him with us. Completing the engine room was hardish (every team should have one) Steve Agnew, hard (every team should have one) Bally, and then a sort of forward line consisting of Craig Russell, Phil Gray, and Paul Williams. Williams was on loan from Palace, and we were the ninth club of his career, which says a lot. We lacked ideas that day. We could win the ball – with Aggers and Bally in the middle, I would bloody well hope so – but with Ferguson again failing to get into the groove, Russ was restricted to belting up and down the left side, while Phil Gray watched and wondered if Williams would ever control a pass, and if he did, if he would ever find the Irishman with a pass or layoff. Charlton were very little better, but they were at home and thus had a little bit more about them. The team looked as if they knew this, but did not seem to have the heart to do anything about it, and when the goal came, it was as scrappy as it was inevitable. We brought on Mickey Gray for the ineffective Ferguson, and Big Chief Lee Howey for the hapless Williams, but there was still no spark. It was only February, but we agreed that the team had relegation written all over it; we were awful, gutless, and deserved no more than the nothing we got.

It was a sombre journey back to Waterloo, and we decided that we deserved a treat to lift our spirits, so we replaced the tube part of the journey with yet another taxi ride, and informed the driver that we needed to be dropped off at the pub behind King's Cross. He happily informed us that it was frequented by "thieves, pimps, and whores", and insisted on payment up front and a "rolling exit" outside said establishment. Two of us did the off-licence run, while the remainder decided to be brave and get the beers in. The "thieves, pimps, and whores" turned out to be wearing Leicester colours, and were in as bad a mood as we were about football, having just been thumped at Arsenal. Ha, so it wasn't just us that made fruitless trips to Highbury. They provided good crack for half an hour until it was time to share out the carrier bags and head for the station. Unfortunately, we had to walk past the offy on the way, and despite it looking like something out of the Bronx – all wire mesh, and the cashier behind a plate glass screen - one of our party showed distinct lack of moral fibre, not for the first time in such situations, it must be said, and popped in for a half bottle of whisky. The game had been that bad, he said, that we needed more substantial refreshment. Good thinking and well done that man. Make it a full size bottle.

The return journey was the usual combination of drink, song, and recovering enough to be ready for a pint in Darlo before the last bus back home. The Number Twenty 2 (that's how they spell it, honest) is one of my favourite pubs, but they don't "do" football songs. Having been to London and back with a thirst for company, we'd forgotten this rule, and were asked to keep it quiet. There was still time to jump off the last bus for a late one (or two) desperate beers in Bishop, just to round the day off, like. Are you detecting a trend here? Like I've said before, never let the ineptitude on the pitch spoil a good day out.

Coventry City (Jimmy Hill is a w*nker)

To be honest, it's not a place that springs to mind when you're trying to come up with nice towns you've visited when travelling around the land following Sunderland. Add to that that football-wise; it's hardly been a happy hunting ground, as we've only ever won there three times since our first meeting back in 1930. Our last win was back in 1985, when the 1-0 scoreline represented one of only three away wins as we stormed to Wembley in the League Cup, but whimpered our way out of the First Division alongside our Wembley conquerors, Norwich – where we'd also won. Add to that a certain Jimmy Hill and a certain evening in 1977, and you'll remember why Coventry aren't top of the list of favourite clubs for anyone of a red and white persuasion, so boo hiss to them. OK, so I cheered when Nick Pickering set up Keith Houchen's goal in the 1987 FA Cup Final, but you're allowed one glitch in your persecution of a team for something they've probably forgotten about.

… and so, in 2004, it began again. After the summer of Euro 2004, Sunderland's USA tour, the Grim Town UK tour, and five new faces, the old season slipped effortlessly into the new season. The Durham Branch renewed acquaintances with folks we'd not seen for, ooh, the couple of weeks since the last friendly. Same bus, same driver, same old (slightly older, actually) faces in the same old seats, same moans, same whines, same jokes and yet another picture in the papers of an Iraqi guerrilla in a Mag shirt. The same A1, same roadworks, same hold-ups, and the now customary tour of suburban East Midlands which precedes every game we play at Coventry, as the driver attempted to convince us that he's never been near the place before. A trip down a couple of cul-de-sacs combined to produce a journey time of four and a half hours to Hinkley, our chosen spot for a bit of R&R. There can be few residential areas of the East Midlands that haven't been graced with an impromptu visit by the Durham Branch. We had so much to catch up on, we didn't even bother with the usual game of cards, choosing instead to be conned into Ronnie's patented (and very complicated) North East football prediction game "all winnings to be distributed and spent during the promotion party at West Ham". We'd have to wait and see on that one, but as far as I can remember, nothing ever came of it and it fizzled out in a flurry of disinterest as the season progressed. Individual moods and opinion on our fortunes in the coming season ranged, as they do in any group of fans, from the insanely optimistic to the suicidally pessimistic.

All of this nonsense followed us as we roamed around Hinkley, deciding which boozer suited our needs the best. Being August, it was ridiculously hot and sunny, so we settled on the beer garden of the pub at the end of the street. It was so good that I've forgotten the name of it, which isn't like me at all. If they're good, they need remembering for next time, and if they're bad, they need to be remembered for next time so that we can avoid them. Common sense. The pub in question had an outdoor indoor games set, if that makes sense. Giant chess, giant, draughts – that sort of thing – but sadly no giant dominos and a normal sized pool table. Our pre-match fun culminated in a "Connect 4" challenge – on a five foot high set, with pieces the size of saucers – while we soaked up the sun, and the August 2004 champion was Ms Owens of Hetton. We turned down the offer of a game of Kerplunk when it was explained that pool cues would be used as sticks, but we did find a way to prevent Rob from having "one last one", as he usually decides to do when we have to leave in two minutes time, by providing beer in a three-pint glass. That, we thought, would teach him. It didn't.

So, on to Coventry, past the pubs designated "visitors only", where optimism seemed high, and into Highfield Road. Like Luton in the cup a few years previously and a few years since, it is scary to think that this ground, the country's first all-seater, was only a few decades ago regarded as the cutting edge of sports stadia. As time had moved on, it looked horribly dated, and provided our last chance for a victory there as the new ground was a rapidly growing tangle of steelwork a few hundred yards away. Thankfully, the pub that we'd used on previous visits was now nothing more than a flat piece of tarmac, and was all the better for it, to be honest. A couple of years earlier, a Boro supporting mate had warned me off the sandwiches there, telling me that the one he'd bought was so bad that he'd stuffed it down the back of the radiator. You've guessed already, haven't you? Yes, we went in before our game, sought out the radiator in question, and found the offending (literally) sandwich.

The weather was much like last year's opener at Forest, but the more open nature of our section meant less fainting and sweating as the usual suspects renewed acquaintance with each other. I had to spend an inordinate amount of time explaining that my scarf had indeed been retired. Its physical health had been commented on several times over the course of the preceding season, and I'd finally accepted that it wasn't really a lucky scarf, just as my original Levi jacket hadn't really been a lucky jacket. Hell, the jacket hadn't even been at Wembley in '73, but the scarf had and thus there was some credence to its claim. It wasn't in a glass case, and still isn't, but sitting on the bus in safety – I couldn't bring myself to leave it at home after all these years, and I needed something to use as a pillow on the way home. It's in a safe place in the back of the cupboard now, but still not beyond another trip to Wembley should the opportunity present itself. So off we went, and Coventry went off as well. The first half was a fairly toothless affair, with most of the excitement coming from the debate between those who sang for Reid to give them a wave, and those who would happily have shot him, had not the Gateman spotted the AK-47 up the shirt and confiscated it. Me, I didn't clap him, I didn't boo him. Had he left us when we were seventh top with a Keegan-esque admission that he could improve them no more, then I would have clapped. On the other hand, I enjoyed the good times too much to boo.

It was a bit disappointing to see only Stephen Elliott – the new Kevin Phillips, we were told - of the new boys start the match, and, while he strove manfully, neither he nor Marcus Stewart gave their keeper anything to worry about. Stephen Wright, he with the lugs to make Dickie Ord laugh, George McCartney, Gary Breen, and Ben Clark on a rare outing, were the defence that would promise us promotion that season, and loanee Carl Robinson, John Oster, Jeff Whitley, and Hoolio the midfield that would make sure of it. Looking back, that was no midfield at all. OK, we know that Hoolio could play a bit and that Robinson could pop up with the odd crucial goal, but Whitley was never going to be a playmaker. His subsequent admission that he was whacked out on Scooby Snacks and Smirnoff for his entire time on Wearside explained a lot, and John Oster had all the skill in the world, but no heart for a battle on the field. The first half was dull, as if both sides were getting used to the heat, and produced little. The second half was livelier, but, with Robinson having one of his defensive days and our wingers looking pretty but unproductive, our midfield provided the forwards nothing to chew on. Coventry's one weak point was the nine-foot centre half Calum Davenport, later of good old SAFC for a handful of games, who won everything above six feet, but had boots of clay. Needless to say, we steadfastly refused to play the ball around his feet and force him to turn, and he only looked troubled when Kyle came on and bumped him around a bit. His central partner,

Richard Shaw, on the other hand, hardly put a foot wrong, and produced several timely challenges to allow the goalie to keep his hands in his pockets.

A fairly even contest, with us having more of the midfield ball and our opponents looking more dangerous on the break, was heading towards an acceptable, if frustrating, 0-0, when George had his absent-minded moment, gazing skyward and losing control to let Coventry in. One quickly became two, which was tough on Pooooom, who'd made several top saves.

So, another crap start to a season, and it was hard to take many positives from this one. Lawrence and Whitehead looked like they meant business, but weren't around long enough to be effective. The forwards got too little good service and showed poor movement and lack of understanding, while the midfield – well, I've already talked about them. Central defence was the area where we looked decent, with both Clark and Breen turning in assured performances, so I decided that they should share my man of the match award. OK, I know I should have worked a little harder to create a differential and decide on one individual, but if the team can't be inventive, then why the hell should I bother?

The biggest smile of the day came on the way home, when we put the film on and discovered that at least six people on the bus knew all the dialogue of "Blazing Saddles". So we mimed and mimicked for a couple of hours, adding a few catchphrases to our matchday vocabulary that we still use to this day, and a lot more than six people know the entire dialogue of Blazing Saddles. Slowly, smiles returned, despite being mooned at by two hairy-arsed Mackems on another bus – you can beat our team, but you'll never beat any sense into us.

Midnight, and back into Bishop market place, where it was all squashed burgers, swearing contests, peeing in shop doorways, vomit, and lasses trying to fight lads. I hadn't the heart for a pint, despite the younger bairn being on duty. New season? It was like we'd never been away.

is also for Crystal Palace

O n our '95-96 train journey down to the smoke, we sat near a group of very smart looking ladies who were on a shopping expedition. They were dressed up to the nines, reading "Bella" and eating Marks & Sparks salads. Our gentlemanly questioning revealed that they were on a regular excursion to London from Tyneside to do a bit of "upmarket" shopping. They wished us good luck for the match, we wished them happy shopping, and, at King's Cross, we went our separate ways, expressing sincere hope that we would met up on the homeward journey.

We met up with Reg, then based in Ross on Wye, who had travelled with the his usual pessimistic outlook – every time he and his brother John, based in Cheshire, succumbed to our gentle persuasion and went to an away game, Sunderland lost. They must have gone to loads, then. John couldn't be persuaded along to this one, although Reg was easier to convince. The usual few beers in the Lamb were followed by a last-possible-minute train journey out to the capital's southern suburbs. Our reluctance to leave the Lamb resulted in a sprint to Selhurst and no time for further refreshment before the match, which isn't a bad thing as it's a good ten minutes from the nearest watering hole.

We went to the window assigned to selling tickets to away fans, where no amount of persuasion could convince the youth behind the glass that three £14 tickets did not cost £38. No wonder they're going bust. Eventually, we stumped up the £38 he wanted, and then had great problems trying to get together exactly £12.6666666 each to cover the cost. We got through the turnstiles, spent the money we had saved on tickets on three of football's better burgers, and raced up the steps towards the seats. The second the field came into view, Nigel Martyn let the ball bounce off his chest for the first of many times that afternoon (he must have been wearing a bullet–proof vest), and the eventual outcome was a penalty.

Not even in our seats, and the chance to go one up at the home of one of the better teams in the division! A cracking start – magic, no less, and we hadn't even had the chance to see who was in the team. Unfortunately, Scotty's spot-kick hit the foot of the post and flew along the line to safety. Bugger, so let's see who Reidy's picked this week. Chamberlain, as expected, Dariusz, the unfortunate Scotty, Mary Melville, and Dickie Ord at the back, midfield of Bracewell and Bally in the centre, Mickey Gray on the left and Martin Smith roaming about behind Phil Gray and David Kelly up front. We generally outplayed Palace without creating too much in front of goal until the second half, when we were awarded another penalty. This time, Le Brace took responsibility, and proceeded to serve up one of the worst penalties of all time. Well, until Jeff Whitley in the play-offs a few years later – against Palace. The thud of the ball into the advertising hoardings lives with me still. Eventually, Martyn let another shot bounce off him, Bally whacked it back into the middle, and Mr Kelly scuffed the ball just inside the post for one of his all-too-rare goals for us. Celebrations of the enormous variety were enjoyed with Sunderland-supporting ex-Mag Kevin Scott who we had spotted close by. We won the game, we eventually won the league, but we missed a hatful of penalties that season, with just about everybody in the first team squad having a go from the spot at some stage.

One nil at Palace – not bad at all. I know people who've been to Selhurst a dozen or more times and not seen us win, so I never let them forget the match that they missed. We headed back to Victoria, where we went to the nearest watering hole for a celebratory pint or three. I forget the name of the pub, but it had a big notice stating that no football supporters were allowed in. We duly buttoned our coats up to the top, and entered. It was half full of lads wearing huge, smug, grins, and coats buttoned up to the top. These were the followers of the day's successful teams. The other half of the clientele were lads dressed identically, but with glum expressions, and were thus obviously the followers of the day's unsuccessful teams. Reg was especially pleased, as his journey across the country had, for once, been rewarded, if not with a brilliant performance, then with three good points. We endured the stickiest pub carpet in the country – a heady combination of beer, powdered glass, unspecified vegetable matter, and straightforward glue (dripped from the noses of the locals, no doubt) – and some of the scariest toilets in the capital, for an hour or so. We phoned everyone who had turned down our invitation to join us and had a quick gloat, until Reg headed for the west, and we headed for King's Cross.

Now, we were happy and suitably "warm" (Bishop Dialect for a having a gallon on board) for the journey home, but our female travelling companions really put us to shame. These elegant lady shoppers of this morning had been transformed, in a matter of six or seven hours, into the harridans from Hell. Mascara down the cheeks, smudged lipstick, hair adrift, holes in their stockings, and heels off their shoes. Blouses with the buttons done up out of sequence, tabs all round, and raucous, cackling laughter. Copies of "Playgirl" and ready-mixed Gin and Tonics had replaced the copies of "Bella" and the Marksie's salads. Harrods carrier bags littered the aisle and balanced precariously on the luggage racks. Our beers lasted until Doncaster, but their G&Ts ran out before Peterborough, so it was off to the buffet car for the girls, lurching down the carriage to the amusement of all aboard. They joined in our now-customary cacophony of "football hits of the 70s", and generally made us look like model citizens for the duration of the journey, despite our vain efforts to drink draughtflow beer straight from the can. Try it; you'll see what I mean.

If ever you have train tickets booked to London, and the match in question is called off, I would recommend a shopping trip instead. It looks to me like it would be an acceptable alternative.

 is for Derby

Way, way, back in time, when I was but an apprentice at travelling away, despite having been learning my trade for five or six years, we had a chance to go to Derby. Well, it was November '76 and I was officially an adult, but Derby was still a long way away according to my Mam.

Despite being based on Tyneside for educational purposes, my Sunderland starting-point for such trips was still very much based in South West Durham, so it was back to Bishop for the bus. I told Mama I was going down the street, as we referred to the cultural epicentre of Bishop back then (still do now, actually), for a quiet pint with some schoolmates who were back for the weekend. Which was all true, but I just got up a bit early and legged it to Cabin Gate for the pickup and the compulsory crates of beer. I now know that there were many and various buses available from Tyneside to the rest of the country, but nobody at Uni was quite of the same mind as me when it came to the football. We travelled by coach with the lads I'd latched onto as a spotty youth a few years earlier, as I felt a real affinity with the older lads who had looked after me as an even younger and spottier youth than them. I still see my guardians from those days, and they're not that much older than me, but when you're sixteen and chasing a pint, an eighteen year old with his club cards is the best mate you could want. As an example of how football can influence society, Lol Bell is somebody I still regard as a guardian angel because of his reassuring presence during those potentially dangerous days. He was looking after our bus for this game, and almost immediately after arriving in Derby, we became separated from the rest of the Shildon and Aycliffe lads. Too much Brown on the way down perhaps? I was too young to decide. The atmosphere in and around the Baseball Ground in the mid seventies was a million miles away from the fairly friendly situation around Pride Park that you find these days, and we toured the neighbourhood in some trepidation as we searched for our companions.

The area around the ground was fairly run down (he said, being very generous to Derby), and we eventually came across a backstreet boozer from which came the familiar sounds of football fans in song, so we cautiously entered, half expecting a smack from some Rammette. What we did get was a chorus of cheers as we opened the door – not for us, but for a well-known Shildon gent who was entertaining locals and Red 'n' Whites alike by riding a very small child's tricycle around the pool table, throwing in the occasional (unintentional) stunt trick before alighting and allowing play to continue. Where he got the bike from we'll never know, but I doubt if it was ever the same again, as he is a fairly big chap. I won't say who it was by name, but if you're from my neck of the woods, you'll know this Frank Zappa lookalike.

The Baseball Ground itself ended its days like Roker Park – dated and redundant – but was a formidable, compact, stadium then. It was covered on all four sides, quite a novelty in the days when away fans were expected to occupy the nastiest, most decrepit part of the ground, and with the crowd close to the touchline, it was an intimidating place for most. Not, however, for our young left back. Ladies and gentlemen, I give you the one and only Joe Bolton. Younger readers unfamiliar with Joe's style of play should think of Stuart Pearce, Mike Tyson, and a bit of Ghengis Khan mixed in with Ollie Reed, and voila – Poker-Face Joe. His expression never changed, whatever (or whoever) he was doing at the time; Vinnie Jones was a flower arranger by comparison, and there's not a player in the poncy Premier League of the 21st Century who could make Joe as much as blink. John Terry? Pussycat. Joe's adversary that day was a Roker character of the future, Leighton James, who was exactly the type of opponent Joe loved – a skilful, fairly fast winger, and more than a bit of a workie-ticket. The kind of player the opposition fans loved to hate.

With Siddall having recently replaced Monty in goal, Joe had fellow calm person in Mickey Henderson alongside him, and Jeff Clarke and Big Jim Holton in front. A midfield of Rowell, Kerr, Ray Train, and Tommy Gibb backed up a front two of Billy Hughes and Bob Lee, so we thought we had a chance. With Rowell having only one goal to his name so far, we had no inkling of the hundred to come, but we had high hopes of Lee and Hughes being enough to get us at least a point. Leighton James had a typical game – he teased, taunted, and goaded Joe; virtually inviting him to clean him out and thus win an early bath. Not one to disappoint, Joe duly obliged, until the contest came to a head in the second half. Leighton held up the ball in the corner-kick quadrant with his back to play, wiggled his arse at our fullback, and Joe predictably clattered him a beaut. In the book, Mr Bolton, said the ref. Five minutes later, and the Welsh Wizard repeated the trick. Joe hurtled towards him with the usual blank expression, with only the experienced Bolton-watcher noticing the steam coming from his ears and recognising it as a sign of his murderous intent. Luckily, one such experienced person was Billy Hughes, who had seen this play before, and knew what was likely to happen in the final act. Billy, a teetotal, non-smoking Scottish lay-preacher, happened to be close enough to get both arms around Joe and haul him away from the inevitable foul and possible custodial sentence. With much finger-wagging, he explained to Joe the error of his ways. Two minutes later Hughesy got himself in the book by continuing Joe's good work and flattening Mr James. I think I saw a smirk on Joe's lips at this, but it could have been a trick of the light. I'm sure that Joe would have been substituted shortly after that, had our man on the bench not been Roy Greenwood, as the boy Roy was famously not the tackling type and a swap for Bolton would have been unfair on the rest of the match. The only time I can say with any certainly that I saw Joe smirk was immediately after an unfortunate clash of heads with well-known Irish radge-packet Terry Cochrane at Ayresome, but that's another story. I met Cochrane (the nutee, I think he can be referred to as) at a charity do some years later, and asked if he remembered poker-face Joe. He did, but with little of the mutual affection that is normally exhibited between ex-professionals.

 **is for Everton**

There can only be one candidate for this one – the Jimmy Hill game in '77. We've all ranted on about this one for years, but how the hell could they hold up a game to wait for Bristol City's travelling support to arrive when they famously never took more than a tractor-full beyond the city limits? Coincidence my arse that the exact same thing happened in 1997 when Coventry went to Spurs on the last day of the season with their survival in the balance. They held up the kick-off at White Hart Lane because of "traffic problems on the M1". Fair enough, there were traffic problems, but we had travelled down the same road, having set off 180 miles further away than Coventry, travelled a further fifteen miles through central London, and still made the allotted kick-off time. Don't get me started.

Having got that off my chest (again), if we'd got a result we'd have stayed up on both occasions, so back to the story. I had next to no money, so I took up my usual spot at the south end of the Tyne Bridge and stuck out my thumb. Result! A bloke taking his mam to the Everton game, so I was sorted for the whole journey, and had a promise of a lift back for free. Lovely. We parked up near Stanley Park, and were immediately offered to have the car protected by the local junior Scallies. 50 pence up front, 50 pence after the game. I suppose that their offspring are the current Scallies who stand at the front of the free bus to and from Liverpool town centre and charge you £2 for the ride. Progress, I guess. At least the time-honoured practice of meeting up at the pub nearest the ground worked, even if we didn't bother going inside, and I was united with usual matchday mates rather than a rather strange bloke from Wallsend and his mam. Lovely people, don't get me wrong, and many thanks for the lift, but not the sort of folks that I was used to watching my football with.

I don't know if they ever did a count of the number of people going into games back then, but I'm sure there were more than the safety committee would have liked. Officially, there were 36,000 and a few, but if that's all there were, then the ground was never designed to take more than 30,000. I remember being distinctly worried for my safety during the game, as the terraces behind the goal bounced when we bounced, and I was convinced that they were about to collapse. We needed to get something from this match, and memory tells me that we just didn't perform as well as we needed to. Having said that, a draw would have done. With Siddall now established in Monty's shirt, he was protected by Mick Docherty, having a go at right back, Joe Bolton, Jackie Ashurst, and Colin Waldron. Of the Burnley old boys that manager Jimmy Adamson had brought in, Docherty had grown into the job, and Waldron didn't let us down when called upon. Hell, he'd even scored the only goal as we beat Ipswich two months earlier. The less said about Doug Collins, however, the better – most importantly, from my point of view, he wasn't involved in this crucial game. Bobby Kerr was the main man in midfield, with the recently discovered triumvirate of Elliott, Arnott, and Rowell his sidekicks, and Bob Lee partnering Mel Holden up front.

Despite frantic and passionate backing from their travelling supporters, Sunderland didn't maintain their recent form, and it was no surprise when big, bad, Bob Latchford scored. One down at the break, but still forty five minutes to get the goal and point that would make us safe beyond doubt. Even getting beat would have been enough to stay up had there been a proper game going on at Highfield Road, but we all know that there wasn't. Latchford took advantage as we pressed forward in the second half, and scored again. We had Tony Towers, who'd scored four in the last six games, on the bench, but there was no final outing in the stripes for him. Doomed – or were we? As long as it wasn't a draw at Coventry, we'd be safe. Radios crackled along the length of the terracing, messages were passed and misquoted, anger and frustration bubbled up amongst the visiting fans. As we trooped disconsolately away, a Polis was heard to say that Coventry were winning. We got him to radio the station, but they would neither confirm nor deny the report. Doubtless, some typical Scouse joker was having a laugh at our expense. Hilarious, I don't think. In reality, we knew that, despite the fact that the farce 100 miles down the M6 was still being played, we were sunk.

We found the car surprisingly intact, coughed up the remaining 50 pence with a growl, and got the hell away. I sat in silence with my driver and his mam, while the rest of the lads drowned their sorrows in a pub on the outskirts of town just before last orders. They were constantly asked what the score had been, and what it meant. The reply and subsequent explanation seemed to provoke the same response from the locals – "Dat's cat dar is" ("How unfortunate and unjust", apparently). They also referred to the barmaid as "Caddle", which sounded like a strange name, until they realised that anyone else would have said "Carole". I think that Scouse must be the least understandable accent in Britain (apart from West Auckland) unless you've had a lot of practice.

Five amongst thousands of near suicidal fans decided that enough was enough, and pointed their Hillman Avenger first east and then north on a seemingly endless journey home. My lift dropped me at the Swan House roundabout, and twenty minutes later I crawled through the window in Jesmond at some ridiculous hour to find my room-mate cowering behind the desk with a butter-knife in his hand. He thought I was a burglar, apparently. No-one took the Michael in lectures the next day, most people being surprise that I'd come back at all, let alone got out of bed. We cursed the big-chinned offspring of Beelzebub to hell and back, condemning him to wear the Black Stetson of the bad guy for all eternity, and wishing a plague of ridiculous bow-ties upon him. At least one of our wishes came true.

There's only one in Fulham

1972 and my first trip to London for the last game of the season. I secured a day off the milk-round, and caught the midnight express bus from Aycliffe, much against the wishes of my Mam, who thought that I was way too young to be heading off for the Smoke (the place, not the tabs). We arrived at Victoria around 6:30, and at 7 o'clock decided to go sightseeing. We looked like a couple of extras from "Oliver" as we wandered around, clutching our little packets of bait. We cautiously got the tube everywhere, although, in hindsight, it would have been quicker, cheaper, and easier to walk.

At that tender age, you don't realise that maps of the Tube aren't drawn to scale. Sightseeing over, we arrived at Craven Cottage early (very early), and paid to get in the open end, assuming that, as there was no roof, it was where the away fans would be expected to go. We were the only ones on the terrace at this hour, and our scarves were fairly conspicuous. We spotted a dozen or Sunderland fans in the opposite end of the ground, and our hearts sank – we had got into the home end by mistake. We approached the stewards, and asked if we could walk around the pitch to the other end. No chance, lads, you'll have to go out and pay to get in again. More expense, but we entered the other end safe in the knowledge that we would be among friends. We duly joined up with the lads we'd spotted from afar, and who we quickly discovered were from the London branch, and were, erm, how can I put this? Shitfaced is a more contemporary term that springs to mind.

Realisation dawned slowly upon us as we looked back across the pitch, and saw that the end we had recently vacated was rapidly filling up with, yes, you've guessed it, Sunderland supporters. So there we were, scarves away, and standing emotionless, as you did in the seventies when you were only little and stuck in the home end when you were away from Roker. Standing in the wrong end, we were protected by our new "friends", who turned out to be as mad as shit-house rats. They couldn't have cared less if they got a good hiding or not, and it was probably this attitude which persuaded the home fans that these unusual visitors were not worth tangling with. Anyway, we survived, and the lads gained a point from a 0-0 draw, largely thanks to the usual heroics from Monty, and a less than usual central defensive partnership of Pitt and Horswill – hell's teeth, that pair, and Mick McGiven in midfield, must have scared the dinner out of the Fulham forwards. (Question - have we ever had two gingers in the team at the same time since then? Answer – yes, Corner and Wallace in the 1985 League Cup Final). With Malone and Bolton, making only his fourth start, also at the back, it's no wonder Fulham couldn't score. Porterfield, Kerr, and Tueart completed the midfield, and Dave Watson was still a centre forward in those days, alongside John Lathan. It wasn't a bad end to a season that saw us finish fifth, but we could have done so much better

England were playing West Germany at Wembley that night, so we decided that another Tube journey would be a good idea, just to get a look at the place. Little did we realise that only twelve months into the future, we would be there as part of one of the greatest sporting events the old stadium was ever to witness. Although we had no intention of going in, as our bus left at 10pm, we were tempted by the offer of tickets at £1.50 apiece from a tout on Wembley Way. At those prices, he wasn't much of a tout. In we went to watch Moore, Hurst, Ball et al. England lost 3-1, and we didn't see all of the goals because we needed to get back to Victoria for the bus. Had we been older and therefore dafter, we'd have stayed right to the final whistle and only then worried about getting home.

First football trip to London, and I had seen all of the sights, watched the lads pick up a point, survived the home end, and seen England at Wembley. Not bad going, really. When I got back to good old County Durham at six in the morning, I was greeted by my bleary-eyed Mam, who hadn't slept a wink all weekend, so worried was she that her little boy would come to some harm in big, bad London. She needn't have worried, I'd been perfectly safe the whole time.

 **is for Gilliingham**

In September 2004, thanks to what has become a traditional England game early in that month we had ten days off "proper" football, then came back with yet another date in the long-distance love affair between the fans and team of SAFC – an affair which of late, had degenerated into one of dull, stale, familiarity that is more like a marriage that has run its course than anything that continues to be passionate. We'd only won twice in our opening eight games, so this was the time for things to change. Despite trouble with the law during the week – Sunderland young guns going for it with a pellet gun, and my narrow escape from arrest in B&Q last night (there I was, minding my own business in the gardening section, when this bloke in an orange pinny walked up and asked if I wanted decking, so, naturally enough, I made sure I got the first punch in) – and a leaky lavvy ruining my bathroom floor and kitchen ceiling, we made the early morning rendezvous. From a 6am start, you can only while away so many motorway miles discussing the news of the week - even the surreal but definitely true (allegedly) stuff, such as:

- Crop circles on the Toon Moor finally being explained when it was discovered that their circumference exactly matched the turning circle of a Toon defender
- Toon chiefs rocked by yet another sex scandal when Keiron Dyer was found taking part in a one-in-a-bed romp
- Craig Bellamy expected to be out for a few weeks after being bothered by a troublesome calf – it wouldn't leave his hotel room until after breakfast.

- until you remember where you're going, and what time you're likely to get home afterwards.

The sort of rubbish mentioned earlier can keep you going for a while, along with the obligatory quiz, crossword, horoscope ('today, Virgo – "there's a 1 in 30 chance that it's your birthday" says Gypsy Rose Tracy-Lee Molpurgusio') or arguments about the manager's tactical awareness, Sven's sex-life, and the weather, but then the sad reality dawns on you that it's Gillingham you're bound for, one of England's truly crap towns – but it gets even better, oh yes it does – the town authorities won't let you in until after 1:30, so you have to stop off in Gravesend (a bit like Wallsend with the good bits removed) where there's no coach park, so it's a running drop-off and a wandering pick-up. This generally takes place near the railway station, so there's the obvious option of a 20 minute train ride into Gillingham to get one over on the authorities, but we thought "why not make like a tourist and find the best bits of Gravesend, however aptly it's named?" Certain members of our party opted for the first option, just to show it could be done, and were consequently oblivious to the events on the field.

Having thought this thought a few days before the event, being of the "planning" kind, and having been dumped in Gravesend last year without a clue as to the location of any decent hostelries, and not trusting my usual innate ability to find a good pub, I'd scoured the internet sites that needed scouring and found that the 2003 CAMRA (that's "Campaign for Real Ale" to those who prefer your drink ice-cold and fizzy) Pub of the Year was the Crown & Thistle in Gravesend, not that far from the station, and boasting views over the Thames to Tilbury, if that's anything to boast about. While I'm quite good at finding these places by using my patented home-made maps, they tend to leave the other lads with the facial expression you see on a dog trying to work a computer, but finding the best bits of anywhere looked unlikely when we passed Gravesend and Northfleet's ground for the second time. "How man Stan, I think we're lost" was the cry, at the very obvious presence of the same football ground we'd passed twenty minutes earlier. Some on the bus even claimed to have been present at the 1962 FA Cup draw there, so they should have recognised it. Eventually parked up in a handy lay-by, we took on fuel at the first available bar, where the "smooth" drinkers were treated to a pint of vinegar. Most of us had the foresight to employ the usual tried and tested method of drinking in an unfamiliar establishment – have a little sip to see what it's like before hoying it down your neck. Not so Ben, who took about half of it in his first sup, then asked if it was supposed to taste like that. The look on the barman's face answered his question in the negative. The more discerning drinkers amongst us made the day's short trek to the above-mentioned Crown & Thistle, and, for once, "Pub of the Year" lived up to its reputation. We watched the Thames flow by as we discussed the tactics which would be best employed by manager McCarthy, noted just how huge

Tilbury docks were, then soaked up the sun out the back for a while. We also remembered that, although we'd only played the Gills a handful of times, they had done something very naughty indeed to us in 1987, and therefore were deserving of a good thrashing. The rain on the way back to the bus dampened our spirits, as 90 minutes in the Scaffolding Stand in the wet did not seem a very attractive proposition.

Of course, we were there in time for a swift one in the Railway Arms, where we spotted Look North's Jeff Brown, making a very bad attempt at being impartial, and who deserves an Oscar, an Emmy, a Golden Globe, and probably a MOBO (Mackem of British Origin) award for keeping such a straight face when he does reports from outside Sid James. We only took a couple of minutes of his time, probing for inside stories, but he could give us nothing that we didn't already know.

Luckily, the weather turned fair, the sun put his hat on, the promised new stand was still at Ikea, and it was £24 to sit in a builder's backyard. We were located right at the back, with only a mesh fence between us and a lengthy drop into the Brian Moore Refreshment Area (I kid you not). The size of some Sunderland supporters was a real worry on such a flimsy construction, and when the team actually gave us a performance to get excited about, the whole place shook. The rest of the ground wasn't that much better, and the "G" had fallen off the team's name on the stand to our right. Illingham Town. There was also a loon in a Boro shirt to our left who decided that he'd spend the entire match trying to make us cry. Carrying on the nice theme, the lads went crazy. Against form and habit, we scored in the first few minutes thanks to good work by Arca and McCartney down the left. They repeated the act ten minutes later for the goal of the game, with Elliott flying in to head home, and we'd barely clammed down when Stewart popped in the third. Game over, and from then on the only thing that could have prevented a Sunderland win was the grass disappearing. I don't know who laid the pitch, but they should have either nailed it down, or bought some grass with roots. Every tackle made one of the strips of turf lift like a loose carpet tile, and by the time Stewart stole a rotten back-pass and rolled in the fourth to complete his hat-trick, it really did look like someone had randomly dropped pieces of turf onto a pitch-sized patch of bare earth. Breen and Caldwell were rock-solid, McCartney ran their right side ragged along with Hooolio, whose touch and control was breathtaking, bringing back memories of the halcyon days of Gray and Johnston. Wright actually came back from injury looking match-fit, and Whitehead impressed in a midfield that also included Carl Robinson and Jeff Whitley. We even had time to bring on Simon Johnson, on loan from Leeds, for the first of his five deeply unimpressive games for us, Mark Lynch for the fifth of his deeply unimpressive thirteen games, and John Oster. The appearance of young John signalled the departure of George, who couldn't understand why we were paying wages to someone with so much talent and so little heart.

Were we that good or were Gillingham that bad? Yes on both counts. They only had two players up for the game (a goofy bloke called Roberts and Andy Hessenthaler), despite having Banks in goal. Their midfield provided no service whatsoever, which Roberts chose to counter by running his socks off. Byfield, on the other hand, chose to counter it by doing precisely bugger-all, confirming what Rotherham fans warned us of – if he doesn't fancy it, he doesn't do it. Well rid of, I think, and maybe the fact that one of his five goals for us the previous season was against Gillingham had persuaded them to sign the lad. They were pretty poor, but what can you expect from a town with a pub called "The Call Boy"?

What a difference a game makes, and for the first time that season, the homeward journey was amongst generally excited and happy people, and not the usual suicidal squad. Coming out of the ground, some Gills fans asked who the number 11 was (number 11? Johnson – haven't we been here before?), as he "looks a real class act" they said. I noted to myself to find out what manner of hallucinogenics were popular in Kent but to be fair to the lad, he'd only just met the other players, and he did look quite quick.

Even Lilo Lil mark 3, the self-inflating deluxe sleep-aid, made her maiden appearance to cheers rather than jeers, and the driver made up for the unsolicited pre-match tour of Kent by getting us back home before closing, despite an unplanned cross-country A1 to M1 switch. It's lovely when you can look people in the eye as you enjoy your pint without having to plan a witty riposte to whatever comments they chose to hit you with after a defeat.

Grimsby

As a town, you can well understand where the "Grim" bit came from – a bit like Scunthorpe, but more politely stated. Our trip here was during the glorious charge towards the Premiership in 1999, when winning away from home was a regular, happy occurence. It was also a family affair – two blokes, teaching their three sons the ways of the travelling Mackem, like the apprentices we were back in the 70s. Our first lesson to them was what to do if you lost your ticket - never a problem in the 70s, as all away matches were pay at the gate jobs. Anyway, a nameless adult member of our party (choose any one from two, and it wasn't me) managed to lose the important half of his ticket, so our first port of call was the ticket office. While one of us had a discussion in the car park with Gatesy, centred on the perils of trying to outshout the bingo caller in the Working Men's Club in Shields, the other managed to negotiate a free replacement ticket with no hassle at all. Full marks to Grimsby ticket office for that one.

Once that little problem was solved, we headed over the railway and, on reaching the sea; turned right for Cleethorpes (some of the Shildon lads turned left, and found Grimsby harbour not too picturesque). We voted the promenade the most dog-turded place in the world – our bracing stroll along the seafront passed through a mile long doggy-jobby minefield. There was also a mad dog, that barked at and chased every passing train – what would it do if it caught one? We headed for the big wheel, guessing that the shows would be near the town centre. This big wheel, however, got smaller as we got closer to it, and turned out to be no more than ten feet high. In fact, the whole fairground was in miniature. The ghost train was a man shouting "boo!" at puzzled three-year-olds in a go-cart. Cleggy itself was a trip back in time – stand-up comedians were on every corner, gaining inspiration for their next seaside landlady gag.

We passed up a pint in the shocking pink Barcelona Tavern, well out of place adjacent to the Victorian railway station, and found the Irish pub to be the chosen meeting place of the Red and White Army. Prices forced our second pint to be in the Buccaneer (cue terrible Captain Morgan jokes) across the road, before we passed the mad dog on our hopscotch back up the prom to the ground. If Cleggy was possibly in a time-warp, then Blundell Park certainly was. The "garden shed" song could have been written specifically for it – it actually looks like one from the visitors' turnstiles. They'd built a temporary stand – at least I hope it was temporary – to house the less fortunate visitors, but we were lucky and had seats in the proper part of the ground, behind the goal. Andy Marriott made his debut, as Tommy Sorensen was still a bit dizzy after his concussion at Bradford a few days earlier, but the rest of the dream team was intact – Makin, Gray, Melville, Butler, Summerbee, Ball, Clark, Johnston, Quinn, and Phillips. Just listing those names makes you feel good. Well, it works for me.

Handy Andy kept us in the game long enough to get our act together, prompting a rendition of "swing low, sweet Marriott", then the second half came, and the Lads were kicking toward our end of the ground. Goals from some ex-Mag and SuperKev prompted some weird celebrations, in the form of a number of soft toys being lobbed onto the pitch. This bemused the stewards to such an extent that they allowed the perpetrators of this crazy event to walk onto the pitch and collect Sooty and Co. Twice. It was also one of those games where we knew that if we were patient, we would win, simple as that, and that knowledge makes for a happy and humorous away following. It was the day when "we're on our way", which had been bumbling around the terraces at away games for a few weeks, really took off, but the best songs came from some 70s throwbacks. They gave us timeless classics like "you'll never take the Fulwell", "from the banks of the river Wear", and of course, the Vic Halom song, before moving into the 90s with "you're shite, and you stink of fish". Which was nice and true. I've always had a thing about Hull and Grimsby smelling of fish, and even after the alleged regeneration of these places, there's still a bit of an odour about them. Some of the locals admit that this is the case; others get quite defensive when the subject comes up. The last time I came across Grimsby fans was at their defeat at Burton Albion in 2010 which ensured their relegation from the league (we had a spare Saturday before our game at Wolves, in case you're worried about my loyalty) when they were in less than jubilant mood. Some gallows humour was on show that day, but most memorable was the scariest-looking skinhead I've ever seen. Apart from doing a Paul Hogan trick with a particularly noisy police dog by pointing at its eyes and saying "calm down", which, to the amazement of the dog-handler, worked, he wore a T-shirt with the slogan "we piss on your fish". Which makes you think – do they?

This was no way to build character in our young apprentices. Watching the Lads wasn't supposed to be that easy, there was supposed to be misery and heartache at every turn before any success and enjoyment came along, especially away from home. That's what made us the fair-minded folk that we are today. We did show them where to get chips on the way back, though. As usual, Wetherby was awash with Sunderland boys stopping off for chips, a quick pint, and the chance to nip into the offy. The kids looked on in amazement as lads filled lemonade and coke bottles with vodka to bypass the "no drinking on this coach" rule. We didn't have to worry about that one in our apprentice days, when a trip to Humberside would have been at least a ten–crater, with a couple of those crates being of Lamp Oil in case of emergency. Emergencies seemed to happen after every match, in that some of us got a thirst on before we stopped for a night out in Northallerton. We explained to the kids that it wouldn't always be that much fun, but it was perfectly within our rights to take every bit of good fortune – and good football - that comes our way.

is for Huddersfield

Back to September '72 for one of our first real (i.e. not Boro or the Mags) away games. We decided on train travel, bought our half fare tickets (for about £1.50 return), and once aboard, headed straight for the buffet car. A small can of Brown was 48 pence, at a time when a pint cost around 12p, so I'm told. Bugger. These exorbitant prices, coupled with the low wages in the distribution side of journalism and dairy products at that time, ensured a virtually dry trip.

We followed the big lads from the station to a pub near the ground, where we secured a half apiece, and sat on the wall outside. This wall dropped a good eight feet to the yard below, where the pub's two boxer dogs lived. To our eternal delight, we quickly discovered that these brainless animals would chase anything dropped near them- and I mean anything. We amused ourselves for a good while, watching several items being eaten for the second (or third) time that day, until the mounted police arrived.

The travelling support had been in general good humour, and everything was hunky dory until my mouth got in the way – spotting a policeman on a white horse, I gave a loud cry of "hi ho Silver, awa-a-ay!" Everyone on foot had a good laugh, and even the officers on the brown horses managed a smile, but the Lone Ranger certainly did not. He leant towards me and explained in no uncertain terms what he would do with his truncheon, should I dare to attempt satire again. As his truncheon was the size of an industrial broomshank, I decided that comical backchat was unwise. Eight months ahead of that famous day in May '73, seven of the Cup Final team were on show, with Billy Hughes on the bench. The match itself was a half-decent affair, as we didn't lose, and Ian Porterfield scored with a shot over his shoulder from somewhere near the halfway line. In true Sunday morning style, the centre half left it for the goalie, who in turn left it for the centre half, and the ball dutifully floated into the top corner. A particularly large Sunderland fan celebrated by throwing me what seemed like nine feet into the air, but forgetting to catch me on the way down. The effect on my ankles was such that I spent the rest of the match hopping from one foot to the other in some kind of manic rain-dance. The bloke drives taxis around Bishop now, so I take care not to give him too large a tip in case he gets over-excited. Despite the classic strikeforce of Dave Watson and John Lathan, we couldn't improve on this, while at the back, Keith Coleman, wacky Jacky, Tricky Dickie, and Mick McGiven kept Town at bay on all but one occasion. McGiven took his defensive duties a little too seriously and got himself sent off, which made for a nervous finale, but we hung on. Actually, I think it's fair to say that both teams hung on. Two months down the line, temporary new boss Billy Elliott would decide that Watson might be a decent turn at centre-half. Well done, that manager.

With a 1-1 scoreline at the final whistle, it was scarves away, in true 70s tradition, and back to the station hopefully incognito. We had time to kill before our train came in, and had to share the waiting room with a group of Town fans drinking "ale" (Huddersfield slang for Newcy Brown, apparently), and talking very tough. As this was before '73, when Sunderland gained huge popularity in all parts of Yorkshire except Leeds, we kept as inconspicuous as possible by saying nothing and smiling sweetly. When our train arrived, we duly climbed aboard, expressing relief as the doors closed and we began to roll along the platform. Passing the waiting room, we spotted the aforementioned Town fans, and hailed them in the time-honoured fashion with the usual gestures and taunts. Fifty yards onwards down the platform, and not yet clear of the station, the unexpected, but inevitable, happened. The train stopped, we exchanged glances of horror, and looked out of the window, back down the track. Sure enough, heads popped out of the waiting room, exchanged glances of glee, and set off at speed towards our carriage.

Now, I'll never know if this is true or not, but I'm convinced that the Casey Jones in the driver's cab knew exactly what was happening, and thought it was a big joke. Just as the Huddersfield raiding party arrived at our carriage, the train slowly began to move away. As the station, complete with fist-waving Yorkshiremen, receded into the distance, we breathed a sigh of relief, and decided that, on future train trips, silence would be maintained until we had crossed the city limits.

is for Haddock... and Hull

Hull can't be left out – it has been such an important part of the footballing education of my generation. The place is just like Blackpool – only two hours away, a crappy old ground, always a big travelling support, and a great night out. OK, I lied about the night out, and (as the song went) it smells of fish, but there is always Northallerton or York for refreshment on the return journey. They might have a shiny new ground now, and you still get the chance for a nice stop-off in York or Beverley on the way down, but I'm sure there's still a pervading piscine odour. So many things have happened on Hull trips over the years - Gary Rowell's first league goal, courtesy of a slow, slow dive by Geoff Wealands in the "pussycats" goal, or 3,000 people with hangovers on New Year's Day 1990, courtesy of an 11am start. There were stupid kickoff times then as well – can there have been any reason to start a New Year game at that ridiculous hour other than to catch "morning after" drink drivers? No, I don't think there was, and as far as I know they didn't catch anybody, so yah boo sucks to the Polis for that one.

Anyhow, back to November 3rd 1973, when we travelled on the "beer bus". Come to think of it, all football buses probably all called themselves that back then, as they all had beer on board. Presumably the famous Wingate Branch kept all of their beer on one side of the bus, resulting in its famous permanent tilt. A combination of a mobile bar that opened at Scotch Corner and our relative drinking inexperience meant that one pint of Brew Ten in a rugby scrum of a boozer in Hull ensured that Boothferry Park was the first ground I ever saw in stereo. The 17,000 crowd was 10,000 up on their average, and most of those extra folks were supporting the boys in red and white. If the day had started well, with a few beers and an enjoyable chat with Laurel & Hardy, the two Polis who always seemed to be on away coach duty when we came to town, then it was downhill all the way to the final whistle. The team Sunderland announced would probably have cost us a fine had we been in danger of actually winning anything that season. Bob Stokoe obviously had an eye on our game the following Wednesday – away to Sporting Lisbon. Having won the home leg the previous week, but at the cost of an away goal that would ultimately prevent certain European glory, the team of Monty, SuperDick, Bolton, Watson, Horswill, Young, Lathan, McGiven, Belfitt, Guthrie (in midfield, I ask you), and Bobby Mitchell (making his solitary first team start) didn't exactly set our pulses racing for the right reason. At least we had Ray Ellison on the bench –'nuff said! Hull didn't enter into the spirit of things, including future Sunderland signings Roy Greenwood and John East Hawley (still an amateur), and duly stuffed us 2-0.

Hull had a novel early 70s method of keeping the opposing fans apart, consisting of a large piece of plywood across the corner of the ground. We occupied the whole of the side with the railway out the back, and various other secret spots, but there was, as ever, hell on where the two sets of fans were closest. The rules were that the home fans could abuse, taunt, and fling missiles at visiting fans, but a scowl in the opposite direction meant immediate intervention by the law. Hull also had a typical early 70s fan, a fat lad with a Northern Soul jumper – you remember the type, black with a big yellow star on the front - and when their second goal went in, he went crackers. The lad obviously lived under the stairs six days a week, and was taken on a leader to the match on a Saturday. He pointed at us, screaming something unintelligible and dribbling down his chin while he leapt around like a maniac. We responded in the time-honoured fashion, and were immediately pounced on by the waiting Polis, who informed us that any more pointing at Hull fans would result in summary execution.

As we trudged back to the bus, a dispute between the two sets of fans attracted the mounted police, who duly galloped straight over our feet. The response of some young Hull lads brought a similar response to that which had attracted the law inside the ground, and we found ourselves once again under the threat of arrest. We eventually hobbled back onto the bus and set off for Northallerton and a quiet night out. The over 20s headed for the WMC, and the younger set shot into the first quiet pub we could find. Recognising our accent and miserable faces, the landlady revealed that her husband was a Sunderland supporter. "Has he got back from Hull yet?" we enquired. "He couldn't go," she replied "he flew to Portugal this morning for the match." What a hero! We left in awe, to find solace at the Young Farmers' Disco in the Town Hall, where, to our delight, every young woman in the area had congregated, intent on finding a bloke. Unfortunately, they wanted a bloke with a big farm, and our city-slicker charm only worked on a few of the less fussy. I eventually found myself in the clutches of a particularly attractive daughter of the soil, and was just explaining the crop rotation method I favoured on my smallholding, when our shop-doorway clinch was interrupted by her brother threatening to take a shotgun to me. He looked the part, with his sensible brogues, screw-on flat cap, checked waistcoat, and tweed jacket – straight out of the Fast Show. As I couldn't produce the deeds to a farm, and was wearing a red and white football jumper, he deemed me unsuitable breeding-stock (the fact I wasn't related to his sister probably had a bearing as well), and the suspicious shotgun-shaped bulge in his jacket was all the proof I needed that farming and his sister were not for me.

We had barely stumbled back onto the bus when most of North Yorkshire Constabulary boarded, and announced that we were all under arrest, courtesy of the disappearance of a sheepskin coat from the club. Searching the luggage racks, they found, among the sleeping bodies, the coat in question, which, we reckoned, must have been thrown in through an open rooflight by the thief when making his escape. Realising the impossibility of identifying and extracting the guilty party, the law sent us on our way. No sooner had they got off than one of the lads dropped his keks to reveal a pair of tights. "I don't know how they got there" he protested, and I doubt if the original owner was likely to complain to the police that she'd allowed a Sunderland fan to remove her tights and then put them on himself. Whatever turns you on. Safely back on the A19, we found a couple of crates of Maxim to speed up the last leg of our homeward journey – the perfect end to a perfectly normal day.

 is for Ipswich

Ipswich is not only a long way away, but it's even further down the back roads than Norwich, with the consequence that to keep moving at any pace at all you need to go just about to London and back. Therefore any excuse to make the journey more interesting and relaxing is gladly taken. Back towards the end of the 2004-2005 season, Mick McCarthy's Red and White Army had built up a head of steam that had seen us climb to the top of the table and have promotion well in our sights. As Ipswich was the only away game I'd ever had a ticket for and missed due to sleeping in (despite quite a few near misses), we decided that we'd have a weekend in Suffolk with a tent, or in a cheap hotel, or under a hedge, and Ronnie offered to drive. Job sorted, holiday time. Well, it would have been, had every available bit of accommodation in that part of England not been unavailable, if you know what I mean. Just when it looked like we'd be in for another start at daft o'clock on a Sunday, the jungle telegraph (John at work) let it be known that the Aycliffe Branch were making a weekend of it, and there were spaces.

Gerrin! Ten days to go, and we were sorted. I spoke to Aycliffe's version of Stan the Man – it must be some sort of benefit to be called Stan if you organise football buses – and we arranged to exchange monies before the night game at Wigan. I'm not sure if you can remember that game at Wigan, but we took about 7,000 and had the whole side of the ground. "I'll be on a Classic Coach" said Stan. Great, I thought, no problem. Until we got there and saw that there were about thirty Classic Coaches, all exactly the same colour. Nothing else for it than to wander carefully along the ranks of vehicles until I saw the tell-tale puff of smoke and there he was. Monies exchanged, we duly won the game and kept the promotion bandwagon very much on the rails.

Despite a slight breakdown at home against Reading, we were still atop the league and looking unlikely to be dislodged. It was no more than a minor setback/hiccough/blip/aberration/day off, that was all, and we had a whole eight days to get our collective heads back together, accept that it was only one game, and realise that we were still top of the league. How we didn't win a game that we dominated for the most part is still a mystery, but I've been around football, and Sunderland in particular, long enough to know that these things happen – to any team, not just us. On another day, we'd have played worse and won convincingly, so there you go. No need to panic, just send a few prayers Jody Craddock's way at Wolves... and hey, they came up trumps! The artistic one shackled Ipswich's Shefki Kuqi to such an extent that the Finn was substituted (in a huff, which boded well for our visit to Ipswich), and then the unlikely combination of a Coal Cart goal and a half decent display from Jessie-in-Chief Paul Ince kept the Tractor Boys five points in our wake. Cheers, Jody, we thought.

The Thursday before our departure and I'd suffered a major panic when I got home from work to find my season ticket application returned – my usual difficulty with keeping the wrong copies of direct debit instructions. Bollox. Quick correction, dash to the Post Office to catch the last post, and it was off with a first class stamp – bugger the expense, I thought. On Friday, while buying an extra ticket for the Stoke match, I checked and it had arrived safely and been "processed".

So, although we were getting absolutely sick to death with non-Saturday, non-3pm kick-offs, and already having avoided a 5am start on Sunday, we were off on the Great Yarmouth Short Break option, which gave us the rather more relaxed 6:45 am Saturday start. Even this looked to be a bit of a doubt as I made my way home from Titanic Night at the Grand, through a blizzard – snow, wind, the lot – clutching a stuffed pig. I'd gone for the easy option in the fancy dress, choosing an Irish émigré. Thankfully, Saturday's weather was more like normal, and away we went to Aycliffe and the pick-up at the Legion. The reduced Durham Branch – myself, Lee, Ron, and John – climbed aboard the bus load of unfamiliar faces, and we were off. Actually, the faces weren't really that unfamiliar, as I worked with some, been to school with others, knew others from Bishop, and had met the rest at various matches down the years. The hotel can be best described as Nowt Awwa, but was perfectly adequate for our needs, which amounted to a bed and some breakfast. Easily pleased, us lads. Great Yarmouth was bright and sunny, and, being acutely conscious that we had a long day ahead of us and had therefore better take it steady, we tried the Tudor Tavern for a game of pool and a quiet pint, and asked the barman where things "happened" in Yarmouth. "Norwich," was his reply.

Well, there was no way we were travelling that far for a spot of whatever happened, so we nipped off to the match. Yarmouth's ground only has entrances on one side, and naturally it was the side furthest away from where we started looking for the turnstiles. Inside, there were park benches for seats, there was sunshine, and there was a little clubhouse with a barmaid from North Shields. They even let you take your pint, in a glass glass, rather than a plastic one, out into your seat, so we sat we sat catching a few rays, having a pint, as part of a gate-busting largest crowd of the season at bottom-of-the-league Yarmouth, hilariously nicknamed "the Bloaters", against Diss Town (is coming like a ghost town). They had sold out of programmes when the crowd was only 152. True to form, Diss camped in Yarmouth's penalty area for the entire first half, failed to score (even from the spot), and then let one in to send the home fans away happy. With forwards as inefficient as theirs, it was probably manager Robert Fleck who scored the goals that won Diss the Norfolk Senior Cup that season. Suitably tanned, we went back to the hotel, got changed, and nipped out for a curry. On the way, we thought it would be a good idea to have a pint and a game of darts. Maybe it was the Adnam's Broadside, maybe it was the poor quality pub darts, maybe the board was made of steel, but Lee couldn't get the darts to stick in the board, never mind score more than five at a time. We tried doubles, cricket, killer – in short, every type of dart game known to man – without his game improving, so we went off on a wander along the list of recommended alehouses, reckoning that a curry house was bound to hover into view sooner rather than later. Three hours later, we gave up looking for Indian cuisine when we happened upon a rather smart looking Cantonese place. The food was nice, but a bit too nice for post-beer eating, if you know what I mean. Cheap, cheerful, piled high, and mouth-burningly spicy was what we were after, but we happily picked at the high class fare we had placed before us. A couple more pints helped to wash it down, then we headed for our home for the weekend. As you'd expect, the last building we passed on the way back, straight across the road from the front door, was a curry house. Even Lee couldn't force another meal down, so we went for the final option – a quick pint of fizzy hotel beer, off to bed, and Match of the Day on the little TV up on the wall.

How I managed to fall asleep with the TV on and Lee's snoring in the next room having passing ships wonder where the fog was, I'll never know, but Good Morning Britain, or whatever it was called, was happily chirruping away when we roused ourselves. At least the breakfast was decent, although some of our party had decided that, as it was a hotel, and they were residents, they would take advantage of the relevant licensing laws and start the day with beer alongside their breakfasts. I remember a time when I might have done that, (see Shrewsbury later in these stories, for instance) when I was young and daft, but not on a Sunday with four hours to kick-off.

So to the real business of the weekend, and we got to Ipswich in plenty of time, which we thought was a bit of a pointless exercise as the pubs didn't open until the game kicked off. Ah, there were enterprising landlords about, and the first good thing of the day was finding the Station Hotel open at 11, and strangely not bursting at the seams. We'd been wary of this place since discovering that they put 20p extra on a pint when Sunderland (and probably any other team) were in town, and had found a couple of decent pubs in town, one of them run by the lass who used to have the Welcome down the street from me. Anyway, as there were precious few people to get in our way, we had time for a couple of relaxed pints – they were of a scarily muscular brew called Ridley's Rumpus, and they set us up just right for the match. We managed to find our seats alongside the rest of the Regular Durham Branch, still bleary-eyed after their early start, amongst the highest concentration of Polis and stewards I'd seen in a long time, and then the ding-dong began.

With Tommy Two (Myrhe) having succumbed to his dodgy back, Michael Ingham, who had replaced him in the defeat by Reading, made his only league start. Those of you who watched our reserves in the time of Ingham will remember him for being a keeper who was never quite going to make a regular first-teamer at Sunderland, as well as someone who could probably swear more loudly and more often than any other player we've ever had. Breen, Caldwell, Wright and McCartney should have been able to protect the new boy, which, to be fair, they did for most of the game. Carl Robinson, Whitehead, Arca, and Liam Lawrence ran the midfield, and Chris Brown and Marcus Stewart, back at the ground where he really rose to prominence, banged away at the home defence all half.

Breen showed good composure, apart from a couple of moments of pure madness, and then Stewy's nerve wavered at the vital moment. A penalty, justly given, but in front of the home fans who still thought so highly of him, and he failed to score. A goal then might well have won it for us, but we were not too disappointed with no score at the break. The half-time highlight was the Town fan in the wig and home made black and white shirt with Dyer on the back. I don't know if he was trying to wind us up, but he gave us a real laugh.

The second half started to go all wrong when Ingham came for the ball but didn't collect it, and Ipswich forced it in for a slightly lucky lead. Our tiring front two were replaced by Brain Deane, who we'd signed mainly to stop him scoring against us, and Stephen Elliott. Inspired tactics and it was instant sunshine, as Deane headed across for Elliott's first touch to end up in the net. Sean Thornton had replaced Lawrence, and his glorious red and white boots almost found success with a typical free-kick. Then Arca produced a delightful scoop over Wilnis for McCartney to run on to, and his cross somehow evaded Deane but not Carlos the Jackal Robinson, who stabbed the ball in. There were smiley happy people all over the away end, we were top of the league, heading for the Premiership, part of Mick McCarthy's Red and White Army, and, of course, we were Sunderland. The scoreboard and clock mysteriously went blank at this stage, then George allowed Wilnis to make his only winning tackle of the day, they were back down our end, and it was 2-2. Then the scoreboard came back on, the ref conjured up five minutes of added time, we held on, they held on, and a point was much more use to us than them.

In reality, we could have won this one three or four one, as we missed a couple of good chances in the second half, but we'd have taken a point at noon, so we settled for the point at two o'clock, especially with the prospect of listening to the Mags being put to the sword on the radio on the bus. They didn't disappoint, failing 4-1 against Man Utd in the FA Cup, following hard on the heels of a 4-1 thumping by Sporting Lisbon in Europe. As the traffic was a bit on the hectic side to say the least, the bus pulled over at a little foody pub, where the barman thought all his Christmas's had come at once, as we asked "do you mind if forty-odd of us come in and spend a couple of hundred quid?". Sitting in the sun, pint in hand, we watched the other Sunderland buses, including our usual trusty charabanc, so we waved and held our glasses high in acknowledgement. Suitably refreshed, we set off for the last leg and as we got further north, the Mags began to pass, each carload greeted with the jeers they deserved. Just for being hard of thinking, that is.

A nice weekend and all we had to do was to win and hope Ipswich didn't, and promotion was ours.

sle of Man?

Back in '84, the temptation of £85 each, including the ferry, for a week's B&B, with the bairn going free (at thirteen months, he didn't eat more than one pie a day anyway), coupled with the chance to watch the Lads' pre-season tour, was too much to resist. We duly blagged a lift to Heysham with Grandma and Grandad Sobs (with a day out in Morecambe as bait), and found, to my delight, that we were sharing the ship with the Lads, and Carlisle United. The mood in the red and white camp was fairly upbeat - despite needing a last day win at Leicester to be sure of safety, those two points had shot us up to 13th, and new manager "loopy" Len Ashurst had actually bought players we had heard of. Howard Gayle wasn't aboard, but we were treated to close ups of our other new boys, and it was interesting to judge the character of the players by their off-field manner – Benno chatted to everybody, and Clive "flasher" Walker spent the whole time in the casino.

Rodger Wylde was making a passable impersonation of the intelligent, widely travelled elder statesman of soccer, but Barry Venison plagued the life out him by constantly flicking the Times that he was reading, and generally acting like the cheeky teenager that he was. Steve Berry was fairly anonymous, which just about sums up his career. I sent the bairn across to the Carlisle team to kick Alan Shoulder, but he picked the wrong man, and gave former Roker hero Jackie Ashurst a good welly. Thankfully he didn't go for their manager, Bob Stokoe.

Also sharing the boat was Paul "Hi de Hi" Shane, who was booked on at the Villa Marina, where he followed Ronricco (the world's greatest hypnotist – he told me to say that) and preceded the all star wrestling and Larry Grayson. To make it a real camping holiday, the only other show in town was John Inman in "pyjama tops" at the Gaiety Theatre. Thankfully, the pubs opened at 10.30am, and stayed open until 11, or even 12 at night, so we sought entertainment there.

The best part of the week was that all of the supporters (Blackburn, St Mirren, Carlisle, us, and Athlone Town) stayed in Douglas, as did the teams. This meant that the fans drank with each other and the players – a particular favourite with the players was the Lion Bar (honest). We shared our breakfast table with two young lads from Wearmouth Colliery who had saved all year to get there, despite the strike, and happily fed young Gary his Weetabix all week.

Game one was against Carlisle on the Monday evening, up the coast at Ramsay, and the bus trip there provided the only instance of less than good-natured behaviour amongst the fans. The bus was free, and fans of both teams were aboard, engaging in good-natured banter – apart from one young Cumbrian in the front seat. He'd obviously got full of beer, and spent the first half of the trip abusing everyone who wasn't wearing a blue and white scarf, much to his girlfriend's embarrassment. He spent the second half of the trip in stony silence, after being told, by fans of both persuasions, that unless he ceased and desisted in his moronic behaviour, he'd be coming into sharp contact with a dry-stone wall fairly soon. We arrived in Ramsay in time for a swift couple in the Bridge Inn with our new-found Cumbrian pals, and then on to the big match. Mark Proctor equalised a goal from Malcolm Poskett, and Gordon Chisholm popped up with a last-minute winner. Good start to the footballing part of the holiday.

The next morning we duly turned up at the playing field above the town, near the brewery, for a kickabout with some of the Carlisle lads, and found that Blackburn, St Mirren, and Athlone had a similar arrangement. So began a week-long series of fantastic 84-a-side matches – does anyone remember who won any of them? Were pre-match stimulants supplied by St Mirren's star of the future, a certain Mr McAvennie? Does anyone care?

Game two was in the Douglas Bowl, which, unbelievably, is the island's premier sports ground. It had three empty sides, and a knackered stand on the fourth, where 99% of the crowd congregated, having walked through the players' pre-match warm-up in the adjacent field. This was young son Gary's first ever match, and he was more than baffled by a group of female fans who'd taken an instant liking to Benno, and spent the whole match screaming "Gary, Gary". Athlone Town looked like a Northern League team, with a good selection of over 35s wearing grey beards. They played like one as well, with their rough-house tactics leading to the Sunderland bench calling the referee over and complaining that our precious stars needed more protection, as some of them intended to earn a living from the sport. As the second half began, Athlone won a throw in, and, as it was taken, a cry of "get stuck in" came from the Sunderland bench. Westy got stuck in, and seconds later the ambulance came hurtling across the pitch to scrape up what was left of the unfortunate Irishman who'd been the recipient of the throw. That soured Anglo-Irish relationships in the pubs of Douglas a bit, especially as big Col scored our only goal as well.

So, a win and a draw saw us back at the Bowl, in the final against Bobby Saxton's Blackburn on the Saturday. For some reason, we took an instant dislike to Art Garfunkel lookalike Noel Brotherston, and barracked him for the entire match. The proximity of the crowd to the players led him to foolishly confront a couple of his tormentors (author included), but not much else happened on the field. The perimeter fence, which consisted of one bar at a height of three feet proved no match for an active one-year-old, and, after Sobs junior had run onto the pitch for the tenth time, he was rugby tackled by Paul Atkinson, who sat him on his knee for the rest of the match. Probably the youngest person ever to sit on a Sunderland bench. As a goal-free result threatened, Westy mistimed a jump, the ball shot in off the back of his head for the only goal, and the Gore Trophy was ours for the second year running. Young Gaz would have to realise that we didn't win trophies every year, even in pre-season, but it was a decent start to life on the road with the Lads for him.

Homeward bound the next day, and the propeller shaft broke in the harbour, making us several hours late, and having to sprint for the last service bus out of Heysham. Being well-prepared, responsible parents, we had 50p left after paying our fares, so we used this to bribe the driver to drop us off at the bottom of our street to save us the walk from the bus station. Family holidays – you can't beat them.

is for Kilmarnock

I wasn't even going to go to this one, but what with a chance meeting at half time during the game at Hibs the week before, and the certain knowledge that I'd never see Sunderland find another team beginning with K to play against and therefore leave a gaping hole in any alphabetically-biased collection of nonsense, I popped my name on the list. I had been to see Kettering Town play Wycombe Wanderers while working in the south Midlands a few years before, but that couldn't possibly count as Sunderland weren't involved.

So, as usual, my sister turned down the chance of a pre-season friendly for a birthday present on the big day, having been someone who accepted such offers in her teens, but deferred the collection until the first home game of the season proper. She'd obviously gained a bit of common sense over the years, unlike her elder sibling, and I was standing outside Bishop's famous Kingsway ground, sadly no longer used for football, bright and early on August 3rd 2003, ready for the minibus north. Considering we'd just produced the worst season of any team in the Premiership and hadn't won a league game that year, the turnout of several thousand at Hibs had been amazing, but Killie was a slightly tougher proposition when it came to travel. No straightforward trip up the East Coast main line, football, and straightforward trip down the East Coast main line (with optional social intercourse with the Mags' hard-of-thinking crew at the Central Station on the way back). I'd given the map a brief peep the night before down at the Grand, and agreed with Denty the Mag that it was just up the motorway from Carlisle a bit, then hang a left for a couple of miles.

Well, it's not that simple, is it? When then bus turned up, I discovered that the organiser, who shall remain nameless, had gone on holiday and trusted that the bus, and all of the rag-tag collection of travellers, would all remember who was getting on where, at what time, and where Kilmarnock was. As I climbed aboard and nicked the front seat, it became apparent that the some of the West Auckland contingent hadn't been at the allotted pick-up point at the allotted time. So as not to miss anybody else, the driver had decided to leave them for the time being and collect everyone else. Mobile phones existed in 2003 (hell, even I had one, but couldn't muster the strength to carry it that far) but not everybody had one, and on this occasion, nobody had anybody else's number anyway. So we flew through to Sherburn and elsewhere (told you we were a rag-tag bunch), then flew back to West. Sure enough, there were the folks we were looking for, unaware that the times had got mixed up. Not to worry, said the driver, I'll soon make the time up – and he did. By the time we crossed the border, we were back on schedule, and hopeful (or should that be fearful?) of arriving in Killie in time for a good look around, a tour of the tourist spots, a nice haircut, and a relaxed three-course dinner. Then we realised that we had to get almost to Glasgow, or so it seemed, before we hung a left, and then it was another thirty miles and forty minutes to Killie, with our early morning tour of the Land of the Prince Bishops, a total of two hundred and thirty-odd miles. Just like going to London, in fact, but on smaller roads.

All of this nonsense meant that firstly, all of the bait for the return journey was eaten on the way up, secondly I'd take a better look at the map next time, and thirdly, never trust a Mag, even on something a simple as distance. Actually, I should add that when I'd gone to the cash-point the previous evening to withdraw some beer tokens for the Great Scottish Adventure, I'd had some sort of brainstorm and completely forgotten my PIN number. No amount of trying would bring it to mind, so I'd had to borrow enough from Denty, which is proof that there are some decent Mags out there. Maybe he'd enjoyed himself at the Hibs game as our Special Guest so much that he felt obliged to finance my next trip. Who knows? Eventually, we arrived in Rugby Park, in a part of Kilmarnock that was all leafy streets, wide pavements, and those sandstone houses that occur only in Scotland. The first people that I bumped into were the two lads who organise the Durham bus, that I usually travelled to away games on – the two who had said there wasn't enough interest from our branch members to justify putting a bus on. They'd changed their minds about going after the Hibs game as well – isn't it surprising what effect a boisterous crowd of Sunderland fans away from home can have on even the most sceptical of supporters.

A nice stroll into the town centre built up the sort of thirst that a journey of that length usually manages on its own, but which had been sated with a surfeit of Irn Bru. Well, we were going to Scotland, and they'd had a special offer on at Morrisons. The first thing I passed before Wetherspoon's was a cash-point, and, of course, the first thing that flashed through my mind was my PIN number. Typical. Not trusting my memory, I quickly withdrew enough to pay Denty back, and hid it in the back of my wallet. The first person I bumped into inside 'Spoons was Jacka from the Durham bus, proving once again that enthusiasm doesn't take long to build up, even after a season as disastrous as the one we'd just suffered. Along with Jacka's brother, who lived up that way, there was a canny drinking team assembled, and Billy Willis was on a mission to take advantage of every cocktail jug offer in the limited time available. Mission accomplished, if I remember correctly, and I was more than happy with a chance to drink along a row of Scottish beers on handpump. After thirty-odd years of travelling with the Lads, there was still a certain thrill about meeting up with mates and fellow Sunderland fans in far-off and exotic places – and Kilmarnock. It felt great to get the singing gear tuned up again, carrying on from where we'd left off at Easter Road a week earlier.

So the stroll back to Rugby Park was a cacophony of singing, and everyone trying to outdo each other with their less than encyclopaedic knowledge of Kilmarnock FC. We knew that they were the oldest club in Scotland and that they'd played in the first competitive match (we thought), and that a certain Alistair Murdoch McCoist had gone there from Rangers. For some reason, during his couple of years on Wearside, his 8 goals in 56 games, hardly stuff to write home about, had endeared Ally to the Roker fans, and he's still held in high regard in our part of the world. Unfortunately, he'd retired in 2001, so we were a bit over-optimistic to hope for him to put in a guest appearance at the age of forty. Still, we could dream.

Our end of the ground was the usual bouncing mass of fans who had convinced themselves that, after a decent draw at Hibs, we had a team capable of winning promotion, the FA Cup, and the League Cup, as well as Mick McCarthy winning any raffle he chose to enter. Beer and football, the classic mix responsible for so many raised expectations and so often the case in pre-season with Sunderland. Well, we had what was in effect a new manager, as Mick Mac's hands had been well and truly tied when he took over a sinking ship a few months earlier, and a few players to assess, both incoming and upcoming. We had the Poominator in goal, Stephen Wright and George McCartney at fullback, and Ben Clark, one for the future, alongside Bjorklund, who we had referred to as Jocky in a vain attempt to ingratiate ourselves with the locals in the pub, in central defence. We had Sean Thornton, McAteer, Thirlwell, and Tommy Butler in midfield, and Kyle, fresh from his goalscoring antics in Edinburgh with Michael Proctor up front. All that talent and Pompey had stuck five past our hosts a few days earlier. Mind, Pompey had passed us on their way up from the Championship in May.

Ben Clark shot himself in the foot early on when he lost possession and Killie were ahead, which dampened the spirits a bit, but the sides seemed fairly well matched despite us threatening more as Kyle and Proctor mixed mobility and muscle well up front. Indeed, Kyle's blocked attempt from Butler's cross produced our equaliser when Proctor was first to the rebound. We're on our way, we sang, to the Premier, we sang, and we were on our way to a probable win as there were only a couple of substitutions – Darren Williams and Whitley on for Wright and McAteer. We fell behind to another goal early in the second half, then equalised from the spot when Kyle was clattered and Proctor stepped up. Just when it was looking reasonable, Kyle got into a punch-up with one of their lads, and both were booked and immediately substituted. Bjorklund and Butler also left the field, with Marcus Stewart, John Oster, and Craig James coming on. We had high hopes for young Jamesy, as he'd looked the business for the reserves before almost a year on loan at Hibs, where he'd looked impressive in League and European competition. Shame he managed only two competitive games for us, which we lost, before roaming around Darlo, Port Vale, Livingston, York, and Barrow, eventually fetching up at Harrogate in 2009. He got stuck in against Killie, but we'd lost our shape and looked likely to take our second successive draws when the home side hit us with goals in the last ten minutes from Kris Boyd and the marvellously named Danny Invincible.

So a game that had promised so much produced six goals but not enough of them for the boys in red and white, who had made up a good proportion of the 3,634 crowd, and it was a bit of a despondent minibus for the first few miles, until someone reminded us that it was only a friendly, and the manager was just trying out formations and tactics. That cheered us up a bit, as we decided that five hours on a minibus was way too long to stay miserable. We cheered up a bit more when we stopped in one of those small Scottish towns with the wide main street and the low, glum, cottages on either side that you find only in Scotland. Luckily, one of them housed an off-licence, so we asked the driver if we could sneak a couple of beers on board. He explained that not only was it acceptable, but that he considered it compulsory as it was pre-season and we were in the middle of nowhere and that, as there was no toilet with it being only a twenty-seater, he'd have no problem when we needed a run-off stop. Ah, back to the seventies! I continued my cultural experience by stocking up with several bottles of that Scottish speciality, Sweetheart Stout. To be honest, this was mostly because of the novelty value, but also because at about 3.1%ABV it was probably the weakest beer to ever have come out of Glasgow, and as such wasn't going to cause any embarrassing scenes on the bus. Besides that, it gave everyone else a good laugh as they tucked into their cans of Tennent's lager, sadly no longer adorned by the Lager Lovelies.

Several hours and several relief stops later, we were hurtling around the back-roads of good old County Durham, getting passengers off as quickly as possible and marvelling at the amount of rubbish eighteen people can produce in twelve hours. Sweetheart Stout might have lacked alcohol, but it lacked nothing in gas, volume, and whatever else it is in stout that fills you right up. Thankfully, I'd been through my relaxation programme by the time we got to Bishop, and I had room for a few English beers while I found the Scottish pound notes in the back of my wallet and repaid my debt to Denty – with a pint's interest thrown in, of course Bring on the League – we're on our way!

Who the flipping heck's eeds?

It was at Leeds where my wife-to-be, at her second, and penultimate, away game, asked why we were kept back so long after the final whistle. When the car-park began to rain down on us in brick-sized pieces, she said "Oh, I understand now", and that just about sums up what a visit to Elland Road usually entailed. Since that early 80s game, I enjoyed (maybe the wrong word) several freebies thanks to a mate working for a company who had season tickets, but had to forgo that dubious pleasure on one occasion to take the kids. You could get into the so-called family section on the cheap if you had kids, so Nige became my brother in law for the day, I made the necessary phone call, and four cheap seats were duly obtained. This family section contained three Sunderland families, and was right next to the nutters who normally occupy the seats nearest the away fans. These nutters were in a bad mood because the size of our support meant that they had to be shifted. "Security" (bouncers, as opposed to match day stewards) told us in no uncertain terms that they wouldn't get involved if we got jumped, so we'd better shut up and hide our colours. Me and Nige complied, but my two kids wouldn't, causing me 90 minutes of twitchy bottom. My other visits might have been courtesy of corporate hospitality and thus requiring the wearing of a suit and tie over the red and white shirt, but you get free drinks and sometimes meet the players.

My first such corporate visit blew my theory that people in the posh seats would be polite. There we were, in the best seats in the house, just behind locals who threatened violence on fellow supporters who refused to call their own black players "black bastards". I've been around football a long time, but that one did surprise me.

Anyway, back to one of the few bright spots to illuminate the lunatic reign of Mr Butcher, as the Lads took a 2-1 first leg lead to Yorkshire in the "anybody, please sponsor me-Cup" in '93. We arrived in plenty of time, a very smart car-load of three Mackems and two Leeds (well, that's where the tickets came from, and one of them has switched over to us now). We signed into the Captain's Bar, where we mixed with the local business community over a couple of Tetley's, then Pos pointed out the odds offered against Big Bad Don getting the first goal. "6-1. I'll have a piece of that." Using my now legendary powers of persuasion (reference the same odds against Johnny Byrne at Oxford in the '92 FA cup tie, when I'd persuaded Stubber that he would be wasting his money. I got that one wrong as well), I coaxed the cash back into his wallet. Financially reassured, he led the way to our seats, above the corner flag in the end opposite the rest of our fans.

Once seated, Pos swore solemnly that he would remain calm, quiet and still in the event of a Sunderland goal. Right on cue, Owers knocked in a free kick from directly below us, and the Don powered in a near-post header. I immediately turned to give Pos a manly, but restrained, hug, just in time to see his feet fly up through my outstretched arms, and have my ears assaulted by a one-man Roker Roar. On landing, he straightened his tie, and, as he turned to offer his thoughts on my skills as a tipster, we became aware of a phenomenon known as "Mackems in suits". About two-thirds of our section of the ground was punching the air, hugging each other, and generally going ballistic - in a refined, business-man like way. You can see this at virtually every away game – just look in the boxes and posh seats when we score. We'll get in where a draught couldn't if there is a Sunderland game to be watched.

Now that we had established the loyalties of most of our neighbours, and that we were safely separated from the rest of the ground, we could happily repeat the celebrations when Phil Gray charged down a clearance for 2-0. The Captain's Bar at half time was a sea of grinning faces, trying their best to remain calm amongst their more serious Yorkshire colleagues.

Leeds pulled one back, but we held on for a famous win despite Gary Bennett leaving the field on a stretcher. Wembley here we come – beating Leeds home and away was surely a sign that were on our way again. We decided on a couple of celebratory pints before leaving the ground, as this would give the traffic time to disperse, and us time to mock the Leeds fans in our party. As we eventually left the ground, the players were also on their way out, so we joined the throngs asking for autographs. As I was chatting to Benno, a bloke in a Leeds shirt leant towards him and asked, in deadly seriousness, "What happened to the lad who got carried off?".

"Oh, I think he's OK" replied Benno, with a smile.

One of our Leeds pals was getting panic attacks, as he'd never seen real footballers up close before, and like any 35-year-old, was going for as many autographs as possible, so he asked me to help him out. Always one to help out a true fan, I leaned through the crowd around David O'Leary, and eventually caught his eye. As I handed over the programme and pen, I said "Thanks David – can you nip over and get Gary Bennett's autograph, please?" He didn't reply, but if ever a look said "pogue mahone", that one did.

A couple more pints in the Wellington on the outskirts of Leeds with the Red and White Army, who wolf-whistled our suits, was a perfect ending to a perfect evening, and left only one question to answer – why did Terry Butcher travel back in shorts? Suggested answer – he was barking mad, but you already knew that.

 **is for Liverpool**

Away, last match of the 80-81 season – just the place to go needing a win to stay up, as they had just won the top flight Championship for the umpteenth time, and we had been rubbish for most of the season. A big enough problem in itself, but nothing to what faced me (or so I thought). The economic climate prevalent in Thatcher's Britain meant that I was working in Peterhead, but I needed to be at that game. I couldn't very well come home for the weekend only to disappear to Liverpool for the match – well, not without the best legal advice that money could buy, and I couldn't afford it. How was I to appease my football-hating (i.e. born in Newcastle) wife, and still give the Lads my much-needed support?

"Daffodil" I ventured (always a safe bet) over the 'phone, "I'll be home this weekend, and we're going out for the day". "Oh lovely," she replied. "Where?"

We caught the 8 o'clock from Darlo, two among a horde of already well-fuelled red and whites. By York, our carriage was a chicken run for females going to and from the toilet, as they were cordially invited to display their charms for the lads. Her majesty was bursting for the relief of British Rail's finest mobile rest rooms, but steadfastly refused to move from her seat and risk attracting any attention. Two hours later she staggered, cross-eyed and knock-kneed, into the ladies' at Liverpool Lime Street Station, the not-so-happy holder of the new world record for bladder control.

We travelled across to Anfield by service bus, with my wife loudly asking, to the amusement of the Scousers filling all of the other seats, why I had stuffed my scarf up my shirt, as it was the same colour, but for the black bits, as those worn by the Liverpool fans. Into Anfield, and we took our places amongst the tightly packed Roker army, ready to roar on God's children to another season in the top flight. Before the kick off, former Bishop player Bob Paisley received the Manager Of The Year award, to rapturous applause from all around, not least the away end. We hoped that he would return the compliment by instructing his players to perform like a bunch of complete tossers, and ensure we got the couple of points necessary – after all, they didn't need them.

Five to three, all ready for the biggest kick-off of the season, and the good lady decided that she needed the toilet again. A disgusted scowl spread across my face, but sensing another world record attempt could seriously damage her health, I pointed at a light some twenty feet above us. "Look for that on your way back" I said "I'll be standing straight under it". She duly left for her ablutions, and returned safe and well just before half-time, missing only Howard "hamstring" Gayle rattling our crossbar. It was nothing short of a miracle that we were still level when you looked at the teams. They were bristling with internationals from 'keeper to the subs bench. Well, apart from Money, Irwin, Russell, Howie and Gayle, but eight's not bad and we had exactly none. Clemence, Neal, Hansen, Ray Kennedy, Lee, Rush, McDermott, Souness – scary stuff. Well, maybe not Sammy Lee, but you get the picture. Barry Siddall saw plenty of action, but to be fair, those in front of him worked their socks off to keep the reds as far away from shooting positions as possible. With Hinnigan and Bolton at fullback, we had Elliott, Chisholm, and Rob Hindmarch across the middle. I suppose either Chis or Elliiott may have been ostensibly a midfielder for the day, but their defensive qualities certainly didn't go amiss at Anfield. Rowell, Mick Buckley and Stan Cummins finished of the midfield, but with a front two of Alan Brown and Tom Ritchie, we could have been excused for expecting little. We didn't - we expected more, we roared for more, and we got more.

The rest of the game went exactly to plan, with Ferryhill's finest, Stan Cummins, doing the necessary. We brought on Big Sam Allardyce for Chis to keep the Scousers at bay, and fought as if our very lives depended on it. In the inevitable surge and crush that followed Stan's matchwinner, as usual when celebrating a goal from a standing start, the wire part of the lovely Linda's bra was forced through her clothing, hooking itself on the jumper of the bloke in front. This resulted in the subsequent sway catapulting her down the terracing and temporarily out of sight, firmly attached to the back of a rather puzzled Mackem, who thought that his birthday and Christmas had come at once. By the time I'd completed her rescue, and warned off the bloke with the hole in his jumper, the whistle went, and the lads had once again saved themselves at the final hurdle. Bob Paisley allegedly sent a case of celebratory champagne into the

Sunderland dressing room – being from Hetton and loving the Lads, he knew that our rightful place was in the top division. Anyway, for us the game was over, and we trooped joyfully out of Anfield, survival ensured, bra and contents intact, and Linda's voice ringing in my ear as she vowed never to set foot in a football ground again.

 **is for Man City**

The euphoria of promotion had hung over Wearside like cloud of intoxicating gas all summer, and a 3-1 home win over Everton, which included the best OG I've seen scored for us, meant that applications for the first away trip of the 80-81 season were at an all-time high. All kick-offs were strictly 7:30 in those days. Unless, of course, your chairman had been at the front of the queue when big chins were being dispensed – sorry, rant over, back to the story...

Part one of our convoy left the North Briton at 4:30 prompt; the three-car line led, surprisingly, by Pete's fully laden 2CV - that's an inverted pram to our younger readers. The Posmobile (1100 Escort) struggled to keep pace with two-pots Pete, but at least we had an hour start on the second part of the convoy, a mark two MG Midget, held up in Darlo because of work commitments.

Despite our early(ish) start, our early pace was not maintained, and we consequently arrived in Moss Side with no time for a pre-match nerve-settler. In hindsight, this was probably a good thing. A frantic search for a parking-space ensued, with the kick-off fast approaching. The terraces around Maine Road offered nothing but one gap at the end of a line of cars, which I used to form a neat right-angle with the vehicles in the adjoining street (while still maintaining sufficient space for access by emergency vehicles, your worship).

We dashed into the ground, just in time to rendezvous with Sobs, who'd had less trouble parking his (much smaller) car, and watch our attacking midfield of Elliott, Chisholm, and Buckley supply the bullets for Stan Cummins to top up John Hawley's hat-trick in a memorable 4-0 start to our away campaign. With Turner in goal hardly called upon thanks to a really solid game from Whitworth, Bolton, Allardyce and Hindmarch at the back, the others could really cut loose. To be honest, we'd have been chuffed to bits with a draw, and while a win would have been fantastic, 4-0 was beyond our wildest dreams. We have had a few memorable games at Maine Road – the FA Cup tie in '73, the 3-2 game in December '81 when Venison scored, and the 3-2 defeat in '91 that sent us down, but this one was the best of the lot in terms of football.

We returned buoyant to our parking-place, only to find a 12' by 4' space where the car had been. A nearby copper thought it likely to have been nicked, as his patrol car had been at the last home game, when he momentarily left it unattended while he directed traffic. I asked him if there was a remote chance that my carefully parked vehicle could have been towed away by an over-enthusiastic, brownie-point seeking officer of the law. He smiled, and directed us to the nearest police station.

Scarves away, we headed nervously for Fort Apache, the Bronx, passing a curious assortment of houses – one boarded up, the next with a garden full of gnomes, and the next with a brand spanking silver Mercedes out front (nothing to do with the illicit supply of pharmaceutical products, we hoped). The night was illuminated only by piercing white eyes watching our progress from the dark recesses of doorways. The sanctuary of the police station became visible across the wilderness, and, sure enough, there was the Escort, securely anchored in the adjoining compound. When I asked why it had been towed away, I was told that some tit had parked it in a daft place. The aforementioned tit was charged, released, and subsequently fined £24.

Relieved to have regained possession of a way home, we even managed to catch last orders near the city limits. Sobs didn't show up for the arranged pint – the exhaust had fallen off the Midget while still in sight of the ground, making the car sound like a Battle of Britain flypast for the whole 120 miles home. His navigator Shacks (half-Mag, half-biscuit) held the map upside down, and they ended up having their post-match drink somewhere near Bury.

We were £24 lighter but what the hell – it might bankrupt me, but I'd happily pay £24 every other week if it meant we won away from home. Gerrin! We stuffed them 4-0.

is for Boro... erm Middlesbrough

I've never understood why, when it's spelt the way it is, they get referred to as The Boro. Why not The Brough, pronounced Bruh as it is in the whole version of the name? And while we're on the subject, why do those that insist on Boro also insist on Middles-broe?

Because it's a strange place, that's why. Built from agricultural roots into a chemical and steel town in just a few years, with not much happening there before those industries came to the fore. As it is actually closer to my hometown than Sunderland is, it should not provide much in the way of adventure when it comes to travelling there. Well, you should try getting to the place on public transport from Bishop if you think that's the case. Nowadays, I use an organised bus, which takes away the uncertainty, but means a lengthy hold up in either a) a lay-by on the A19, b) the services at Wolviston or c)the car-park at the Wynyard industrial park (for which John Hall probably charges us a fee), and I've even driven a few times – twice to Ayresome Park, which was great fun if you like pretending to drive at Boro Boys after the match, and once to their new place, when I had to park miles away. Back in the day, it was public transport. In all the years I've been going there, I've seen us win twice, and I had to wait twenty seven years for the first one, when Darren Williams headed home Chris Waddle's cross to relegate the Teessiders, and then in September 2005, when Tommy Miller shinned one home in the first minute and Arca wrapped things up in the second half. It's just a shame that we were relegated at the end of both those seasons.

Six months into my apprenticeship as a regular Sunderland follower, it was Easter 1971. Being 1971, when men were men and footballers played as many games a day as possible without fear of either injury or getting a bit tired, we'd played Orient at Roker on Good Friday, April 9th, and seen Dick Malone cement his place in the hearts of Sunderland fans by winning the game with a second half strike of such ferocity that, had not the net got in the way, the back of the Roker would have been knocked down several years before it actually was, and several Roker Enders would probably have been blasted into oblivion with the ball firmly lodged in their collective midriff. Up to the end of March, we had not won in eight outings, a run that ended with a 5-2 win over Swindon the week before Easter, and were consequently below mid-table. What we needed after those two wins was another and the derby (as they called it) on Teesside was where we had to get it. Games against the Boro always seemed to be quite passionate affairs back then – in the first ninety years of playing them, there had been two sendings off, and that was Raich Carter and Ted Davis in the 6-0 defeat at Ayresome in 1936 – a couple of months before we were crowned Division One Champions, proving that it is, indeed, a funny old game. In the forty years since I've been watching, there have been six sendings-off –Kerr, Tueart, Bolton (ah, that Terry Cochrane moment!), Hardyman, Ord, and Makin – so you could usually guarantee a well-contested game.

So, barely eighteen hours after we'd got off the OK after the Orient game, we set off for darkest Cleveland. Our little party of six or seven, with an average age hovering around the thirteen and a bit mark, was hardly what you could call worldly-wise when it came to travelling away, but what we did know was that Boro railway station was strictly off limits. If you went there as an away fan, you could expect to have to fight your way out of the place and all the way to Ayresome Park. There was no organised bus from Bishop that we knew of, so we congregated in Doggart's Café and waited for Pos to make the first leg of his circuitous route from Aycliffe to Ayresome. As we shared sausage rolls and bacon sarnies, and loosened the tops on the salt and pepper, as was our wont of a Saturday morning in those days, we decided that, as the train was a definite no-go until we started at least looking a bit harder than we really were, it was the number one to Darlo then all change for Teesside. An hour later, we were charging from one upstairs front bus seat to another as we made our connection to Middlesbrough. I had a distant relative who lived somewhere on Teesside, and visits to the Reid's house were my only previous forays into that part of the world. By the time we arrived in the town centre, we realised that none of us had a clue where the ground was in relation to the bus station. Following the time-honoured football adage of following the crowd, we worked out which way to go, reckoning that it was safe to display our colours, as this was in the days before our return to black shorts at the behest of Bob Stokoe. So red and white it was, despite the fact that more than a couple of us had customised our scarves by stitching on the names of the players – we were versatile in those days, embroidery was no shame for us lads. Pitt was a particular favourite as there were only four letters, as was Kerr, and as Todd had been until his departure a few months earlier.

As it had been two hours since our Doggart's sausage rolls and bacon sarnies, the appearance of a baker's shop precipitated an impromptu food stop. We asked for pasties, the lass behind the counter asked if we wanted short-crust or puff, and a gang of young teenagers fell about laughing. We might have learned the useful stuff like stitching from Domestic Science and our grandmothers, but nobody had ever mentioned puff pastry before. Despite her bewilderment, she managed to work out that we'd probably prefer short-crust, and off we went, following the crowd to Ayresome and arriving about one. Obviously, that was way too early to be arriving at an away ground, but as we were way too young to be in the pub, and had set off early because we didn't know where we were going, we had little choice. There were, of course, no tickets, and no attempt by the law to direct visiting fans in any particular direction, probably because the law fully expected heads to get broken, and their policy seemed to be to let those that wanted to fight get on with it and only nick those daft enough to engage in a bout of fisticuffs right under their noses. We sort of followed the jungle telegraph, and some of the big lads who we recognised from the Fulwell, and ended up crammed onto a street corner at the junction of the main stand and the Holgate. Naturally, the gates at the other side of the Holgate were opened first, allowing the Boro boys to get in and lob a load of stones, bottles, and various pieces of scrap over the wall at us, taking a heavy toll of house and car windows as well as a few cracked Wearside heads. Our little band were amongst the first wave inside when our gates did open, so we spent the first few minutes sheltering in the turnstiles as the Teesside Artillery continued its bombardment. Had Saving Private Ryan been made thirty years earlier, we'd have made comparisons to the opening scenes, but it hadn't, so we just thought "bugger, this isn't much of a laugh." Once there were a suitable number of big lads in, a semi-organised charge took place, with us, as young apprentices, filling our rightful roles of jumping about behind the big lads and making a lot of noise.

So it was that we witnessed first-hand the phenomenon known as taking the home end, and we stayed about fifty-fifty for the entire game, with the odd skirmish taking place when the crowd surged or someone took a particular dislike to someone on the other side of the front line. There were 26,000 or so in there, as opposed to 42,617 for the home game – and that's not a statistic I ever have to look up, as, for some obscure reason, it's one that has stuck with me ever since. One day, I might forget it, but I don't think so. I can see myself sitting in my rocking chair failing to remember my grandchild's name, but telling him or her that what the crowd was on Boxing Day 1970 at Roker. Anyway, Monty was in goal, as he was for every competitive game that season, with SuperDick, our new goal machine, and Cec switching to left back in front of him. A little and large central partnership of Pitt and Martin Harvey completed the defence, while Porterfield, Kerr, and Gordon Banger Harris made up the midfield. Up front was Dave Watson, yet to be informed that he would turn out to be one of England's best central defenders of all time, alongside Billy Hughes and Paddy Lowery. The first half was just like the Boxing Day game at our place, all attacking, open play and loads of commitment, and it ended 2-2. Another 45 minutes of that would have been great, but the majority of the action after the break was in the centre of the Holgate as the Boro boys tried to claim their terraces back and we stood our ground. "Stand, Sunderland" was the cry, and it was the first time I'd heard that rallying call – and not the last, especially in subsequent seasons at the Boro. Twinkle-toed Bobby Park replaced Porterfield, but there were no more goals, and we had to turn our attention from football to survival. Scampering along the terraces that surrounded Ayresome, we somehow managed to retrace our steps, past the comedy puff pastry baker's shop, and onto the Darlo bus without mishap, then repeated the trick for the relatively safe second leg on the number one.

There it was, our first away game, reached under our own steam with nobody over the age of fourteen involved in the organisation, or lack of it. Thinking back, we were more than a bit lucky not to have got caught up in some of the front line stuff, or been on the receiving end of a piece of Ayresome masonry, but we got a point, we'd been there with the big lads, we'd got home in one piece, and we were ready to carry on our Sunderland apprenticeships.

 **illwall**

No one likes us, we don't care. So they sing in that part of South East London, and they're lying, because they very obviously do care. They genuinely want to be disliked. The Old Den, or Cold Blow Lane as it was sometimes referred to, was a bloody scary place to go, but the move to the New Den doesn't seem to have changed the attitude of their followers one bit. They seem determined that the rest of the football world will dislike them and do everything in their power to make that happen.

Off we went for a Bonfire Night special in 2004. When will the TV people learn that nobody outside Millwall wants to watch Millwall? Judging by the pitiful following they took to Old Trafford seven months earlier for our FA Cup semi-final, not even the people in Millwall want to watch Millwall that much. After the heady enthusiasm generated by a win over Wolves only three days earlier – another reason for not having a Friday game, but let's press on - we were still in a good mood about travelling to London on a Friday. By the time we got there, that good mood had all but evaporated, thanks to the vagaries of Friday traffic on the A1, the M25, and all other London roads. Whichever misguided imbecile at Fixture Buggeration HQ decided that it was acceptable to move this game should have been atop the first available bonfire. Millwall at any time is bad enough, but to expect fans of any club to make a 500 mile round trip on a Friday, just so that Sky can have their match, is pure lunacy and greed.

The traffic problems meant that the back of the bus discussion group had time to dismantle and rebuild the Welfare State, watch a film, an episode of Phoenix Nights, play five games of cards, and rage about the above-mentioned kick-off time. One of the national radio stations had a phone-in during the week, on the subject of "why is interest in football in decline?" Why are people unhappy with the way things are going? A Sunderland fan rang to say that the reason he was peed off with the direction of the game is because of nine away games so far, only two had kicked off at three on a Saturday, which seems a well-put argument. Not quite as well put as the next caller, who said that televised games had to be on midweek evenings "because not everyone can get to the telly at three on a Saturday." The absolute ignorance of some people in this country amazes me at times. We also discussed George's trip to Madrid, which meant that he'd missed the Rotherham game – because the kick-off had been moved. At the Bernebau, he'd been on the tour, in the top row, which is about as high above sea level that you can get in a European stadium, when he spotted a youth in a Mag shirt being photographed in the centre-circle. Speeding as only a man can when having spotted such an atrocity, he eventually cornered the offender in the club shop, only to find he was from Eire, barely knew where Newcastle was, and was about to have "Raul" put on the back.

As we crawled through London, passing the Queen Victoria pub which advertised "shit food served all day", which is one way of ensuring the chef didn't get overworked, Rob managed to squeeze his drink carton and shower himself with vitamin C as we had our customary tour around the Millenium Dome. Eventually parking up in Charlton at 5:30, we once again gave the landlord of the Antigallican a nice Friday surprise. If Sunderland are playing at Charlton he expects, and gets, a cracking session of record-breaking beer sales. If we're playing at Millwall, he expects a quiet evening chatting to a couple of locals. What he got was a busload of thirsty travellers intent on making the most of the limited time available. An hour's power drinking and his holiday was probably paid for. As we trundled along the final few miles to Millwall, every other shop, apart, of course, from Elvis's Chinese restaurant, was a barber's, and everyone was getting their hair cut – at 7 on a Friday night. Strange people, those cocker-nies.

An unusually small convoy of two coaches and a minibus was testament to the effect of the day and time of the match, but those that did make the journey were impressively vocal. There was also some good news for Palestine, as we discovered their next leader was amongst us – Yasser Marrowfat, actively seeking "peas in our time". That's what happens when you wear one of those Shemagh-type scarves to the match. The New Den is a nice ground – far too good for those that inhabit the home sections. I don't know exactly what they were up to, but it was bad enough for there to be a steady stream of ejectees from the part closest to us. On the field, and the home victory of a few weeks back was long gone, as they were back to their niggly, petulant selves. It took only a couple of minutes for Wise, the human equivalent of what comes out of the back end of a Yorkshire

Terrier (a little shit) to have Bridges by the throat, and only a few more to work out that Arca was being targeted. Perhaps the only person in the ground not to see the elbow that flattened Julio was the ref. Basically, they bullied us out of the game, and our new-look defence was pulled all over the shop by Tessem, who is obviously only on loan, as he was their only player to actually try to play football. Wise should have been long gone by the time Lynch added a slightly raised arm to a standard tussle, and it was always going to be given by the ref who proved to be the milkman of human kindness to Millwall all night. In came the text message from our Ian "it was a pen, but Wise is a t****y f****r", which sums him up perfectly. Up the field, our midfield couldn't get a grip of the game, and what chances we did have either came back off the post (Carl Robinson) or were too easily dealt with by the keeper (Bridges). Even after our defence fell asleep to concede an awful second, we still felt that if we could get a grip of the midfield, the game was there to be won.

Well, as you know, they didn't, despite tireless effort from Whitley, which gave rise to the Jeff Whitley song being Top of the Pops for the last half hour. I can't even remember how that one goes, so it can't have been that memorable, just like the player. Bridges, after building up to the game so well, was disappointing, and Stewart just couldn't get into things. The referee could have saved himself an evening's work by just giving the whistle to Wise, because, make no mistake, he was the man in charge of the game, and when the officials let that happen, the opponents have no chance.

So the game fizzled out, or rather Sunderland fizzled out. Our wide men hadn't delivered because the central men couldn't win the battle in the middle and consequently the forwards got negligible service. At the back, Myhre couldn't be blamed for either goal, the central two looked uncomfortable as a pairing, Collins (D) is not a bad player, but not yet comfortable at left back, while Lynch had yet to convince me that he could do any sort of job for us. As it turned out, he couldn't, and started only two more games before he was shipped off to Hull, who shipped him off to Yeovil, who in turn shipped him off to Rotherham. Unbelievably, he scored two goals in one game for Rotherham, out of a career total of two.

A thoroughly downhearted homeward journey was filmless, as there were no Ingmar Bergman films black enough to match our mood. We moaned our way up the road, hoping that we can show some bouncebackability (copyright I. Dowie) in the next game, at Leicester – after all, it was at three on a Saturday – rolled out Lilo Lil, slept as best we could, and got home at half three. I'd had better days.

is for N*wcastle

As with the Boro, travelling the short distance to Tyneside shouldn't present many geographical challenges, and it doesn't. Getting to Sid James Park as a Sunderland fan, however, is slightly more fraught than getting to Plymouth on a donkey with three legs. These days, it is a well-policed operation involving a convoy from Sunderland, or a crowded train or Metro ride. Some brave souls make their own way there by car, because they are either a bit mad, or they live north of the Tyne. It's actually the only away game I've ever walked to, pre-season excepted, of course, and I also tried the car option many moons ago. It was Frank Clark's testimonial, so he chose Sunderland as the opposition, and as I'd just passed my driving test, I volunteered to take a carload up. I borrowed my dad's Wolsey 1885, which was big enough for six, and parked up near the brewery. The turnstile man spotted the spelling of Lucky's Ha'way the Lads badge, and threw a punch at him. He spent the first half with his Levi jacket inside out, and kept popping up at various points in the Gallowgate, to cries of "there he is, with the silver jacket." I can't remember the score, but I do remember that Mel Holden scored more goals than Malcolm MacDonald, and when I got back to the car I found Tubby hiding behind it. He'd been at the Central Station by half time, and had only escaped dismemberment by running along a row of cars to make his escape. Ah, happy days. I drove there from my Whitley Bay home on the occasion of Mr Rowell's finest hour, and I walked to the place when I lived nearby.

In September 1979, I had a birthday, as I had in each of the years since I was born, strangely enough. I was, at that time, living what might be best described as an extreme bachelor lifestyle in the west end of Scumcastle, so Robbo and I jumped on the number 38 and headed to the Theatre Buffet to begin the celebrations in the usual manner. Doris the barmaid might have been getting on a bit, but she was a proper barmaid and she looked after her regulars. My treat was to always be given an oversized glass for my hand-pulled beer, which meant that over the course of a good evening I would end up having an extra pint on Vaux. That's what we had planned for my birthday, but it's not what we got. Having warmed up nicely, we wandered up to Sid James Park for the main event – the second round, second leg of the League Cup against our nearest and not so dearest - watching as the Sunderland Boys marched along the other side of the road. We cleverly employed the commando tactics honed by years of dodging bother at away games (me with Sunderland, Robbo with Scunthorpe. OK, maybe just me, then) and drifted un-noticed past the Polis and into the red and white throng. The chance to have a bit shout and sing at last was the best present of the day so far, and it released a lot of the nervous energy that tends to build up when you're drinking in bandit country, albeit in a relatively safe boozer, and I felt a whole lot better by the time we got inside. Being a night game, it had that heightened sense of atmosphere generated when the darkness takes away any view of the outside world, leaving you only with the football ground and its inhabitants to contend with. It helped that the week before, we'd surrendered a one goal half time lead to draw 2-2, with Wilf Rostron and Pop Robson, from the spot, getting our goals. Perhaps surprisingly considering his antics in our previous game against the old enemy, we'd left Rowell on the bench for that one and we took to the field on Tyneside technically at a slight disadvantage as they had two away goals.

Barry Siddall saw his defence change, as Jackie Ashurst replaced Gordon Chisholm alongside Whitworth, Bolton, and Jeff Clarke. Mick Buckley (in for Arnott), Elliott, and Rostron were joined by Rowell in midfield as we swapped from a three man attack to just the two up front, with Entwistle the man to miss out. Alan Brown and Pop Robson were the men we hoped would score the goals, Rowell was the man the Mags hoped wouldn't. The place was seething, and the noise of the crowd was befitting a first half with no goals but plenty of effort aimed at getting some, and we continually reminded our monochrome chums of the events of February 29th that year. Mr Rowell's name featured heavily, as you'd expect, along with several other less savoury comments on the mental capacity of those who wore the wrong stripes.

Both teams must have realised that the home defence wasn't up to holding on to that away goal advantage, so it went a bit daft in the second period. Two goals apiece, both of ours from Alan Brown – one of six local lads in our team – as he levelled things late on. Both teams went for the win, as if extra time would mean too late to bed for the players. Rowell was replaced by Chisholm to shore up our defence a bit, extra time came and went, and it was still level. There were no fingernails left among the fans, which was a shame, as they would have given me something to chew on during the penalties. It was gone ten o'clock when they started them, and with Rowell having left the field, our number one taker was out of the picture. Still, Pop had done the business from the spot in normal play in the first leg, so we should be all right. Hell, that shoot-out was tense. I think it was the first one I'd seen, and I'd have happily settled there and then never to watch another one. First up was Pop – deadly. 1-0. They scored. Then Wilf Rostron did the business. They scored. Up stepped Mick Buckley. 3-2. They scored. Jackie Ashurst – 4-3. They scored. Steve Whitworth – in again, 5-4. They scored, so it was sudden death. Hell's bells, would it ever get settled? Chis put the sixth in, and they scored. Man of the moment Alan Brown jogged up to the spot and put it away. Then it was the turn of Jim Pearson, who responded to our wishes by missing. 7-6. Gerriinnnnnn! Happy Birthday! Robbo, formerly of Scunthorpe United, was most definitely an honorary Wearsider for the day. The away end bounced like only away ends do when Sunderland have won, every red and white person there was the best friend of every other red and white person there, and there was pandemonium as bodies were flung up in the air in mad celebration.

Extra time, penalties… where would the time for my birthday drink come from? It was gone twenty past ten when we got out of the ground, and the Buffet was five minutes away on a good day. On a really, really, good day, such as one when Sunderland had beaten the Mags on their own turf, there were obstacles in our way. Obstacles such as several thousand locals with murderous intent, and a sizeable police presence intent on getting everyone from the away end to the Central Station as quickly as possible. Very commendable idea from Northumbria's finest, but not much use of you only lived at the end of the 38 bus route, and even less use if you wanted to nip into town for a celebratory bevy or three. We went with the flow a bit, as the Central was vaguely in the right direction, but a few hundred yards from the ground, there was a bit of a scuffle over on the other side of Gallowgate, and everyone's attention moved in that direction. Once again employing those handy commando tactics, we did a bit of a body swerve and got ourselves away from the crowd being escorted stationwards. We jogged as casually as we could, as jogging hadn't yet been invented, past Stowell Street and across Newgate Street, then along Blackett Street and down Grey Street. 10:27 ish, my watch said. Naturally, we got in a double round (each), all in oversize glasses, and Doris asked if I'd had a nice time on my birthday. Too right, pet. Cheers

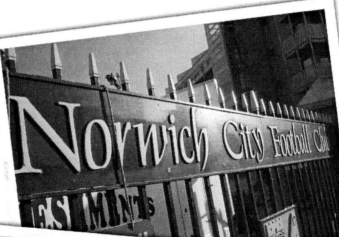

 **orwich**

The trip for the penultimate match of the ultimately disastrous 76-77 season was one of the first for which we hired our own coach, with Pos the man with his name on the documents. After playing like puddings until March we looked dead and buried, until a draw at Highbury, when Bobby Kerr kissed Pat Rice, and the introduction of the unholy trinity of Elliott, Arnott, and Rowell brought us back to life. We were on a bit of a high, as we'd been scoring shedloads of goals at home, and it looked like we could even stage the 1970s version of the Great Escape and stay up.

My day began at about 5am, with a scheduled pickup by Pos Travel at six in Bishop Market place. We walked the streets, growing in number as we knocked up the lads on our way. All went to plan until our last port of call, where Mally was still fast asleep. As Mally often overslept, there was a large bamboo pole secreted down the side of his house, so that he could be roused without disturbing his mam. We duly battered his window until he poked his head out and asked where he was supposed to be going.

Ten minutes later, and the second laugh of the day as our coach rolled into view, emblazoned with the logo "Seagull Travel, Blackpool" – a sub-contract job, as it turned out. Once convinced that it was indeed heading for Norwich and not the Golden Mile, we climbed aboard. It quickly became apparent that this was one of the first travelling casinos in Britain – apart from the usual games of brag and pontoon, and the domino cards, Mick ran sweeps on:

• The distance to Norwich
• The last digit on the speedometer when we got to Norwich
• As above, but for both the return journey and the complete journey

- The time we would get to Norwich
- Who would escape with the match ball
- The time of the first goal
- ....and the age of the driver, to the nearest six months

This was also during those halcyon, civilised days, when you could drink beer on coaches without fear of arrest – in fact, if you were going to the match, it was virtually compulsory. One of the problems associated with drinking on buses in those days was that none of them had toilets, so you either needed an eight pint bladder, a very understanding driver, or something to pee into. The old trick of lifting up the floor panel and wetting the driveshaft was both upsetting to the driver and dangerous, as well as likely to give you an unwanted shower, so we'd given that one up, and brought some plastic bottles. Not very efficient, or sanitary, but better than wetting yourself or holding your tackle in a vice-like grip while trying not to cry. Some of our travelling companions had access, through their places of work, to equipment designed for those members of society who have a problem with incontinence. These marvellous devices were basically a large (3 pints? 4 pints? Who knows?) plastic bag with a little funnel on the top, and they provided instant relief to their owners during travel. The only problem was that they got full, and had to be either emptied or disposed of. The first bag-related incident came when one of the lads stood up to dispose of his bag, and it came away from the funnel, landing right on top of his neighbour's head, and giving him a first-class golden shower. "You dirty b*****d" he screamed, while the rest of us folded up with laughter.

"What do you mean, me?" replied the one with the detached funnel in his hand, "you're the one with pee all over your head!" Cue another ten minutes of hysterical laughter, as the wet one poured copious amounts of Cedarwood aftershave over his head (I can still smell it to this day), and removed his jeans, jamming them in the rooflight to dry.

The next bag-related incident involved the ejection of a full one from the rear rooflight. The timing of this ejection was far from good, and, as soon as it had been hoyed, a red Triumph Spitfire appeared, directly in the line of fire – and, as you might expect, with the roof down. Also as you might expect, but the driver didn't, a direct hit was scored. I vaguely remember it hitting the bonnet, but I was later told that it landed in the bench seat, just behind the driver. Have you ever seen 54 people trying to stay out of sight on a bus, whilst attempting not to wet themselves with laughter?

Despite these aids to continence, we decided on a comfort break by the road in Lincolnshire. The sight of a busload of football fans, one with no trousers, peeing into a field was too much for the elderly couple enjoying a picnic in the layby – especially when the trouserless one had his keks deftly removed and flung into the hedge. They packed up and sped off in their Morris Minor at a totally unexpected speed. The arrival of a red Triumph Spitfire hurried us back onto the bus, but there were 54 of us, and they turned out to be Sunderland supporters anyway, so we were safe.

Nearer to Norwich, the police stopped us and said that we were too early, and couldn't go into town until half past one. No problem to us, we simply went to the nearest roadside pub. Big problems for the roadside pub – they had never seen more than ten people before. The landlord dragged his granddad downstairs to help out, but the old boy had such a dother on that your pint was only a half by the time he rattled it down on the bar in front of you. We boarded the bus with pints in hand, and carrying the life-size cardboard Babycham girl from the lounge. I kept my Watney's Red Barrel glass for several years as a memento of the day, using it for hair-washing purposes, and had to break the damn thing with a hammer when I got sick of it, as no amount of dropping would do the trick.

When we were allowed to park up in Norwich, it quickly became apparent that the local constabulary could not cope with the size of the travelling support. No advance ticket sales in those days, you just turned up and paid on the gate. Consequently, the street outside our turnstiles was a disorganised mass of bodies, with no queues in sight. Lucky decided that the only way to be sure of getting in on time was to climb over the fence, so we gave him a bunk up above the seething crowd, and he duly impaled both hands on the spikes cut into the corrugated iron sheets at the top. As he tried to pull himself up and over, a Polis appeared on the toilet roof, looked down at Lucky, and said "If you come over this wall, son, I'll chuck you straight back out" We managed to push him high enough to unstab his hands, and he fell back into the melee below.

We did all manage to get into the ground before kick-off, along with almost 28,000 others. We even caught the pre-match kickabout, and Swagger decided to claim first prize in the sweep by catching a ball and, very indiscreetly, hiding it up his shirt. This resulted in almost immediate ejection from the ground - seven hours on a bus, a real battle to get in, and he never saw a ball kicked in anger. No match ball, no money from the sweep, either.

Siddall, Docherty, Bolton, Waldron, and Jackie Ashurst made up the defence, with Towers and Arnott pulling the strings as Elliott won the ball and Rowell did the running behind Lee and Holden. It was a bit of a cracker as games go, with us battling for every ball and earning four bookings in the process. Towers made way for Bobby Kerr, and the change proved decisive, as the little feller scored our second after the inevitable contribution from Gary Rowell. That gave us reason to be cheerful on the journey home – especially when we saw the distinctive green and yellow match ball bouncing around the back of our bus, courtesy of some cunning undercover work by Davey Scott. The seemingly endless convoy of coaches was escorted to the A1, whereupon we stopped at the first sign of civilisation – Newark. This happened to be the day that Forest achieved promotion, and Newark's proximity to Nottingham meant that the place was packed with surprisingly bad-tempered Forest fans, leading to several interesting confrontations. Mally discovered that a very effective method of avoiding a good kicking was to fall over and throw up over the legs of his would-be assailants. One to remember if you're ever on the receiving end of such an assault.

Come closing time, our friendly landlord tried to persuade us to leave, but the lads hadn't been on MOTD yet, so no one budged. In fact, we built a viewing arena from the chairs and tables so that everyone got good view of the telly, and we sang our hearts out for the lads for the second time that day as we watched. I hope the cleaners got paid treble time the next morning - they deserved it. We eventually got home around 2am, and if anyone ever found a bait-box with a match programme in it by the side of the A1, I'll have it back, please.

O is for Orient

There are a number of ways to get to the match, and over the years, we've tried them all. Hitch-hike, supporters' bus, train, car, boat (Isle of Man), plane (Watford 1999), walk, cycle, and service bus. The last one is fine for home games, but, based on experience (this one), it is to away games what Seamus McDonagh was to the art of goalkeeping.

Christmas '74 came and went with only four defeats suffered, and 32 points in the bag already. Things were looking decidedly canny for the lads, and, fuelled by the prospect of a promotion campaign and seasonal alcohol intake, a trip to east London on December 28th seemed a good idea. Myself, Tubby (six feet tall, 9 stone), and Sicker (doesn't like the nickname now, but he lets his kids wear N****stle gear, so we can call him what we like) found an overnight bus that picked up at Bishop at midnight, and duly booked up.

We met in the Cumberland around eight, as we were wont to do of a Friday evening, and took plenty of goodies on board, in the form of Ex and crisps, and also a mixture of abuse for missing a late one at the Queen's and respect for going to away game overnight. When the Cumb closed, we headed for the Market Place. We boarded the bus, carry-outs in hand, as our pals entered the Queen's for someone's 18th/engagement/any excuse for a late drink. At 18 pence for a pint of Gold Tankard, we were saving a fortune by drinking bottles of Brown on the bus – sorry, luxury coach. Coaches in those days weren't nearly as comfy as those of today, but, had it been light, and had we not had a drink, I doubt if we would have got on – it looked like a refugee from Beamish Museum. This was the equivalent of the slow train – it stopped everywhere. Darlington, Northallerton, Thirsk, Leeds, Doncaster, Sheffield. At first, we were glad, as there were no on-board lavvies, and we looked forward to each bus station toilet like George

Michael on holiday. Eventually, somewhere on the M1 after another bog-break in Leicester, the bus stopped stopping. In fact, it stopped altogether, knackered, and we had to push it across the car park – all of us, even the bloke who wouldn't put his guitar down – and wait an hour until a replacement arrived.

It was well light by now, and way past breakfast time when we arrived in the capital, so we fed our faces and decided that it was too cold to spend all morning sightseeing or standing around waiting for the pubs to open, and we simply didn't do shopping. We duly checked out Leicester Square, and were delighted to find a cinema "open 24 hours". Being of a certain age, we were doubly delighted to find that the bill was "Maid for Pleasure" and "Erotic Diaries" – two masterpieces of mid-'70s "art-house" film making. We thought at first that we'd get hoyed out for laughing, until we noticed what was going on beneath the bowler hat in the lap of the bloke next to us. We'd have been shot for doing that in the Odeon in Bishop. We shifted seats and watched the remainder of the performance (the bit on the gravestone still looms large in my memory) with one eye on the audience.

Our lust for culture satisfied, we headed for the delights of Trafalgar Square, where we treated the Lions to a slurp from our bottles of Brown, then took the Orient Express to Leyton, where we surprised the locals by having a pie and Brown picnic in the park. Into the traditional freezing-cold open away end, where we were amused by one of our lads constantly expressing his pathological hatred for all things Cockney, including the West Ham fan who'd come to watch us because we were his second team. This London hater sat near me at Wearmouth for a while, and he's a little more mellow now – at least, he is at home games.

As we watched this non-fight taking place (it takes two to tango, as they say, and the West Ham lad wasn't interested), the Lads trotted out with Monty, Malone, Bolton, Moncur, and Dave Watson at the back. Ha, they'd never score past that defensive line-up. A central midfield of Dennis Longhorn (insert crude pun at your leisure if you like) and Bobby Kerr seemed logical, with Billy Hughes wide on the right and Jackie Ashurst – well, let's say he was a centre half – in for Tony the Tiger Towers. Helping out in front of the defence was his job that day, and he did it reasonably well. Pop Robson and Vic Halom (Vic Halom, Vic Halom, la la la la la laaaa) were up front, and we expected great things. We started like we were going to get them, as the game was barely kicked off when Billy Hughes nipped in from the right, and scored. 11 seconds – the fastest ever Sunderland goal? I would think so. Far from being a foundation to build on, the Lads decided it was a lead worth hanging on to. Maybe having three centre-halves on the field lent itself to a defensive game, protecting a lead. Me, I prefer single goals to come as late as possible, so that we don't have to hang on too long. We were still in the first half when ex-Smoggie Derrick Downing, he of the ridiculous sideburns (to narrow it down a bit), lofted in a centre from the left. Consternation on the terraces. The winter wind caught the ball as it flew below us, and carried it over Monty's despairing hands. Panic on the terraces. It then hit the post. Relief on the terraces. Then things got silly – it hit Monty on the back of the head, and flew into the net. Disbelief on the terraces. "Arse," we thought.

The second half was more of a solid defensive performance, with Joe Bolton beginning a run in the defence, and Jackie Ashurst dropping deeper. The Orient fans cried "bring on Cunningham", and out came their bright prospect for the future – Lawrie Cunningham, soon to be of West Brom, England, and Real Madrid. He certainly livened things up a bit, and, by full time, we were happy with a point as he was like lightning down the touchline. Game over, lugs, fingers, and toes numb with the cold, and a light jog back to the tube, and warmth. An hour later, and we were aboard another dilapidated charabanc and off on the slightly more reliable, but no less circuitous, trip back north. When we disembarked at Bishop, we discovered that the equaliser at Brisbane Road wasn't the only thing the wind had got hold of. The remains of the day's market was strewn about, and several roofs had been removed in one piece. The streets were littered with slates, and we were pleased to find our homes in one piece in the small hours as we snuck in without waking the folks.

Service buses to away games? Forget it.

Oxford

Those of you with good memories may remember "plan C" from the Bristol City tale – well, here's how it changed to plans D, E, & F in August '75. Having been half frozen during my alfresco kip in the Bristol park shelter, I decided that a duffel coat over my "lucky" Levi jacket (laid to rest after one appearance at the new ground – you can't argue with a pedigree that included five relegations and three goal-free Wembley visits), and a plastic mac in the pocket. Thus prepared, I got out my trusty thumb, and set off south, allowing a good 26 hours for the trip.

I managed the first 100 miles without a hitch (pun) before spending the obligatory three hours near Doncaster. Around 9pm, a Reliant Scimitar pulled up, and the driver replied "Oxford? Drop you off near there" – sorted! I happily climbed aboard, then noticed two other hitch-hikers, crammed into the back with their man-size rucksacks. Within a few minutes, I came to understand the reason for their worried expressions, as we hurtled south with one wheel on the central reservation, honking and flashing at anyone travelling at less than 120 mph. I stared up through the open sun-roof, watching the night sky flash past, and contemplating my chances of surviving the journey, which seemed pretty slim under the circumstances.

I was eventually dropped off "near Oxford" – I don't know what my driver did for a living, but he was no geography teacher. If you check your maps for Shefford, you'll find it happily nestling next to Baldock, many miles east of my destination. My next lift was with ten West Indians in a Cortina, who listened with interest to my story, and were still laughing when they dropped me in Watford at midnight. I decided I had travelled far enough, and after a wander around looking for somewhere to sleep I eventually spent the night in a cricket pavilion there, emerging, Compo-like, at dawn, scaring the pants off the milkman delivering the wherewithal for the afternoon's tea and sandwiches.

A series of poor lifts got me as far as High Wycombe, where I gave up the thumb after sprinting to an Alfa Romeo with the roof down, only to be beaten into the passionate arms of the driver by his gorgeous girlfriend, who skipped from a nearby house. Looking at myself, I couldn't fault his choice of travelling companion. The service bus was a welcome, if over-budget, luxury, and I felt a sense of relief as the dreaming spires of Oxford came into view as we dropped down the northern edge of the Chiltern Hills.

Despite the team's pathetic antics a few days previously at Ashton Gate, a few pints in the White Swan soon got us back in the hopelessly optimistic mood that usually precedes away games – Tricky Dicky was in for Wacky Jacky Ashurst, and we had three up front in Holden, Robson, and Halom – how could we lose? We had Monty, Malone, Bolton, Jeff Clarke, and new captain Bobby Moncur at the back, so that was a good start. Tony Towers, Bobby Kerr, and a rare appearance for Tommy Gibb made up the midfield. As it turned out we didn't lose, although the pre-match pints combined with lack of food to make me forget Bobby Moncur's equalising goal after we'd been down at the break, and leave the ground convinced that we had lost 1-0. I was eventually convinced of the correct score by Col from school, who I had met in the pub, and who was also travelling by the rule of thumb. We agreed to join forces, but, unfortunately, there is an unwritten law which states that doubling the number of hikers halves the chances of a lift. This meant that we walked for miles around the ring-road, with no sign of a pick-up. We took turns to put our arms out, and, as I extended mine for about the fourteenth time, my fist came into sharp contact with the head of a passing moped-rider. Fortunately, there is an unwritten law which states that doubling the number of hikers halves the chances of a good thumping from irate motor-cyclists.

By 10 pm, we were still liftless, somewhere on the A43, so we pooled our finances and found we could afford a couple of pints apiece in a pretty village pub. We asked if they had any pies, and were told they only had quiche. We asked what that was; decided that egg custard with onions in wouldn't kill us, and duly spent the last of our pennies. Suitably refreshed, we set off again, and met up with a serious hitch-hiker – waterproofs, big rucksack, map, and (most importantly) an endless supply of salted nuts, which he happily shared. We slept, surprisingly well, under a tree on a military camp near Bicester, and I awoke around six to find that Col had set off a couple of hours earlier, so that he could be back in Bishop for his Sunday dinner.

I left my new friend snoozing under the tree, and walked another ten miles or so before hunger forced me to nick a pint of milk from someone's doorstep and gratefully pour it down my neck - sorry, middle England, but my need was greater than yours. By this time my blisters were getting the better of me, and it was with great relief that I accepted a lift to the M1. I'd only been waiting at the junction for a couple of minutes when my next lift arrived. "Hold tight" said the driver, handing me a helmet, and I climbed aboard a Triumph 650 for 180 miles of sheer terror. As my experience of motorcycles was limited to wheelies on Stubber's moped outside school, I spent most of the ride north hanging tightly onto the strap, as my arse bumped a foot above the seat at every tiny bump. I dismounted at the A68 three hours later, my right leg soaked in hot oil, and wobbled the four miles to Shildon, where I met another school friend who lent me 20p for the bus home.

I arrived in Bishop around 2pm, a couple of hours ahead of Col, and in time to cook my own Sunday dinner – no quiche involved.

lymouth Argyle

8 19 miles for ninety minutes of entertainment is a bit extreme, but that's what you get when we play Plymouth. Some folks don't go that far on their holidays, and it means that Friday night is spent on a bus, the toilet of which someone has kindly decorated with their evening's beer and kebab. This decoration is not compulsory, although it happened on more than one of the coaches, and this evening it appeared to contain a lot of beetroot and bright yellow stuff.

As it was early season, August 2004 to be precise, it's always an excuse to have a night out to help with sleeping en-route, and I was lucky enough to have two beer festivals to choose from - the Grand or the Daleside. I chose both, and was heartened to discover that we've signed the Mags' best defender according to the landlord of the Daleside, in Stephen Caldwell. Shame he couldn't keep us a clean sheet. We'd negotiated a bit of a stoppy-back as the bus didn't leave until midnight, and the taxi driver turned out to be an old acquaintance of Ron's. He was on the brink of taking up the spare seat on the bus, but decided against it at the last minute. We arrived a few minutes early at the pick up point to find a good crowd having a beach party outside the long-closed pub – Spanish beer, food, straw hats and Bermuda shorts, the lot. All aboard the Plymouth express. Even the first appearance of my very own super Lilo Lil (£9.99 version) was scant comfort, although it did get me a couple of hours of comfy kip. Sleeping on buses is an acquired skill, with only a select few being competent at it, but some, like Mr Owens, being Grand Masters of the art of falling asleep on a clothesline in less than a minute. Us mere mortals need to take advantage of it being a Friday night.

By the time we called into the giant caravan park that is Exeter services, we felt (and probably looked) like we'd travelled several thousand miles, so it was nice to be able to stick your head in a sink for a couple of minutes to freshen up. However, seven in the morning in the motorway service toilets is neither the time nor the place to be applying hair gel, although Lee did look ready for a night on the town when he'd finished. Shame it wasn't yet 9am when we hit town, but he led the charge through Littlewood's café for the 74-item breakfast. They must love it when we come to town.

Wetherspoon's pubs might be much of a muchness and beer supermarkets, but they're cheap, easy to spot, and some of them opened at 10 back then. When our lass phoned at 11:05 she said "it sounds like you're in the pub already", I didn't have the heart to tell her that we'd been there an hour already, and had been joined by Mr Fickling and Ms Callaghan. They declined our offer of a game of cards, and they showed little interest in Ron's patent North East football prediction league (in which I was currently nowhere, but thanks for asking) so we roped in a couple of young lads from Rickleton, who showed their gratitude by winning money. This was despite one of them wearing a suspiciously black and white tracksuit top, and Lee (AKA Brett Maverick) having ten more cards than anyone else.

Suitably refreshed, we took the number 43 to the ground, squeezed another couple down at the Britannia, a less typical Wetherspoon house, and won Britain's fifth gold medal of the day by winning the repacharge (spelling dubious) in synchronised road-crossing. We thought we'd solved the mystery of the vanishing Irishman Thomas Butler when we discovered a fair-haired youth in a number 14 shirt with "Butler" across the top, and speaking with an Irish accent. The shirt was genuine enough, but had been a gift from its owner to young Eamon, who told us that the real thing was trying to get a contract with a club back in the Republic. Unfortunately, he didn't know what had gone wrong with Thomas's head that forced the disappearance. Full marks, though, to the wearer for flying from Eire to Bristol then skateboarding to Plymouth.

Full marks not to Plymouth, who'd sold us numbered seats and then told us to sit anywhere. Likewise Mick McCarthy, who'd given us numbered players, but then let them wamble about fairly aimlessly for the first half. We had Tommy Two (Myrhe), Stephen Wright, Arca, Breen, and Caldwell at the back, and a funny-looking midfield of Carl Robinson, Whitehead, Liam Lawrence, and Oster, with Kyle and Marcus Stewart up front. By the time most of us had found where not to sit, we'd conceded a sloppy first goal, and spent the rest of the half on the back foot. Plymouth took the game to us, were quick, incisive, and enthusiastic, and we had nothing to counter that with. OK, we came out livelier in the second half, could have had a penalty when Arca was felled, but didn't really deserve anything other than Stewart's consolation. We brought on Stephen Elliott, Sean Thornton, and Mark Lynch for Oster, Lawrence, and Wright, but could do no more than pull one goal back thanks to Thornton's guile and Stewart's awareness. Three goals in four games from Stewart had been a decent start to the season but, on the other hand, if he continued his goalscoring exploits he'd pretty soon become a saleable asset, and we all knew what happened to them.

It's a long enough journey with three points to carry, but a lot longer with none, and our choice of film entertainment summed up our mood – Deliverance.

 **is for Preston**

As young apprentices in October '73, we took the Red Lion bus and watched in glee as the mobile bar opened at Barney. That's Barnard Castle to you, and that's where the bar opened when we were heading to the North West – it was Scotch Corner if we were heading south, as you'd expect. After terrifying the residents and shopkeepers of Kirkby Stephen (they really should have been used to us by then), we parked up in Preston. We entered our first – and only, as it turned out – pub with the usual teenager's sense of wonder. Wonder if we'll get served. Not this time. This time it was different, as my gaze fixed on the game of dominoes in progress in the corner. A sight completely new to my young eyes – nine spot doms. How could you hold enough to play a game? How could you remember more than 28 combinations of spots? I immediately decided that this strange Lancastrian phenomenon should be shared with the rest of the civilised world. Sensing a business opportunity not to be missed, I reckoned that, with the right marketing, I could revolutionise the world of dominoes back in County Durham. I could see so much more potential here than I could with those funny little dartboards with no doubles or trebles that they have in Oldham. Straight away, I formed a business plan – I could nick a set, and return to the North East victorious, bearing treasure from strange, faraway lands, like some latter-day Walter Raleigh.

A half of beer later, and with the future of British sport carefully secreted up my jumper, we left the pub. I decided to nip back to the bus and leave the booty there, for fear of in-ground piracy. We hadn't got fifty yards when I was invited by the Polis to accompany them to the station. Maybe the lump in my canary-yellow jumper had given the game away, or perhaps some vindictive representative of BBC Sport tipped them off. Either way, it was an easy collar for them – none of this "Yeah sure I did it and I tell ya I'm glad I did it" Jimmy Cagney routine. I went for the pathetic Frank Spencer approach, sang like a canary, and with the obligatory clout round the lug for being a daft kid, was sent on my way. The copper who lifted me even gave me a lift back to Deepdale, chatting about the merits of Dave Watson, with me eagerly agreeing with his every word. Mind you, I was that relieved to be going to the match that I would have agreed that Malcolm McDonald was a decent turn and not the cockney gobshite that he was (and still is).

So, with my aspirations of being the nine-spot domino impresario of North East clubland cruelly thwarted by the long arm of the law, I thanked my new uniformed friend and turned my attention to the match. Into the ground long before kick-off, I located my mates quite easily, as they were the group hysterical with laughter, pointing at me and shouting "jailbird". As there was not much in the way of organized pre-match entertainment (no sign of the Dagenham girl pipers here), Shildon's answer to Frank Zappa decided that the home end looked much more appealing than our end, and walked across the pitch to have a look. A brigade of young red and white foot-soldiers followed, but I decided to stay put, now that I was a recognised felon. This was no charge across the field, so typical of the era, but more of a leisurely stroll. Five minutes later, after a bloodless coup, the moustachioed one decided that our end wasn't so bad after all, and led his flock, clutching a few blue and white souvenirs, back to their very own version of the promised land.

As it turned out, Dave Watson was injured and didn't play. Neither did Richie Pitt, whose career had ended in a heap in front of the Fulwell during the home defeat by Luton three weeks earlier. So it was Dave Young and Wacky Jacky Ashurst in central defence, with the rest of the cup-winning team. Easy win, we thought. Wrong, said Preston, managed by Bobby Charlton, and with the still vicious Nobby Stiles patrolling midfield. That was the season that every team saw us as the team to beat, simply because we were the FA Cup holders and therefore a big scalp. Perfectly understandable, I suppose, but of little consolation. We held out for the first half, but succumbed to the only goal of the game after the break. The Lancastrian half of the near 22,000 crowd left happy with a 1-0, the red and white half grumbled their way back onto the buses.

As was virtually compulsory back then, post-match Blackpool was next on our itinerary, but the place was absolute chaos. October, full of the usual Blackpool tourists and fans from every fixture north of the M62, including Scotland. So it was colours away, and the Bierkeller, the Foxhall, the Manchester, and the Pleasure

Beach, in that order. We were ambushed by some Liverpool Scallies outside the shows, and I received a belt in the mouth from one of those walking sticks full of Blackpool rock. Others were less fortunate than I, and bear the scars of that attack by the Rose Garden to this day. As we sat licking our wounds and arming ourselves with pop bottles should our assailants return, an old dear offered us aspirin as if it would make broken teeth return and broken noses miraculously straighten themselves. Nice thought, though. Some Rangers fans had seen the incident, and said they'd watch our backs for the rest of the night, which was a bit of a surprise. We took refuge in the New Brunswick club, watching the "turns" in the deep end. Perhaps tame by Blackpool standards, but at least no-one tried to thump us in there.

Back to the bus, and we fought off (ineffectively) a very persistent pair of Liver Birds in "kiss me quick" hats, one smelling like an ashtray and the other of vodka and lime, as we waited for everyone to turn up. We eventually departed only one man down, which is not a bad score for a Blackpool trip. Somewhere out on the Pennines we stopped for a run-off, next to some roadworks, as the flashing orange lights provided a bit of visibility for the bladder-emptiers. Fresh turnips were plucked from the field for sustenance, and as the bus pulled way, several orange flashing lights appeared from beneath jackets. As this was years before "let's all have a disco", no blame can be retrospectively attached to Terry Butcher, which is a shame, as he has a lot to answer for. So it was a darkened coach, except for our mobile light show, that rattled over the moors, with "Ballroom Blitz" crackling from the speakers. At least we could see just enough to eat our freshly-picked snaggers.

At our first drop-off, in West Auckland, we found the missing passenger standing by the road, hitching a lift. He had no idea how he'd got there, or even that "there" was only three miles from home. A fitting end to an eventful day, and all we had to show for it was a fat lip, courtesy of too much Blackpool rock, and a 9-6 domino, courtesy of the secret pocket in Sobs's scarf. Perhaps the future of entertainment in the pubs and clubs of the North East was in for a change after all.

Q PR

December 1997 saw us play at Loftus Road, where we hadn't won since about 1899, as the media so kindly reminded us at every opportunity. They were wrong on that one, as we'd never won there at all, but we were a month or so into a good run, so we were confident of three points when we headed for Shepherd's Bush. The East Coast main line was by then as familiar to us as the last bus home from Durham, but Sobs was ending a month's work in the USA with a carefully engineered return to coincide with the game (yes, you're right – mad). A 6am arrival at Heathrow allowed him to be at King's Cross in time for our arrival – not that we would have recognised him, every inch the intercontinental executive, had it not been for the A4 sign held aloft, bearing the letters "FTM". We could only admire the sentiment. As we headed up the Euston Road, he morphed into something more familiar, removing layers of clothes like a snake sheds its skin, and replacing them in garments that only come in red and white. Back to life, back to reality.

We had our standard Café Shiraz brekky/blotting paper, and early aperitifs in the Euston Flyer, which would have been even earlier, had the antipodean barman been able to understand English. He thought the tube was something that beer came in. The pub proclaimed "no football fans", but cleverly showed the 11 o'clock game between Liverpool and Man Utd on the telly, great bit of marketing, that. Somehow, they didn't recognise us as football fans, or didn't care. Whatever, it was a nice warm-up before stage two of our trans-London expedition. Being London, the place was full of Man U boys who'd supported them since well before Bryan Giggs, Ray Keane, and Barry Pallister had graced Old Triffid. Typical.

We stuck 45 minutes of this, then headed for our first rendezvous – stage two, the Jeremy Bentham, run by and old pal from Bishop, where the rest of South West Durham gathered, and we could get properly warmed up for the journey out west. This place was known as a "destination pub" – explained to us as somewhere that people actually travelled to from all over the capital for a night out. Probably because the staff spoke real English and it served decent beer. It tends to help if the customers get served what they ask for. After a few pints supped while renewing old acquaintances, we were on the tube, and into a converted card shop on Shepherd's Bush Green, converted to Flanagan's traditional (?) Irish Bar. Here we met up with the remainder of our extended red and white family, which somehow had grown to include a young New Zealander. It was bound to happen under the circumstances, I suppose. She survived a good twenty minutes of concentrated red and white preaching before a pint of Guinness was spilled down her leg. The guilty party, who shall remain nameless but was probably the one who latched onto her in the first place, as he has a penchant for trying to educate foreigners when in London for the match, offered to pay for having her trousers cleaned, as he should. What came next was a bit of a surprise, as she took him by the hand and led him to the adjoining laundrette, where he waited as she removed her keks and had them cleaned and dried (gentleman or pervert – you decide). Needless to say, the happy couple returned to loud cheers.

A few pints of the black stuff later, and it was way past time to leave for the match. A lone fiddler busking entertained the crowds as they squeezed into the School Lane End, where they found themselves behind various pillars and posts. Apparently, some tickets are actually marked "crap view", and the pitch seems square rather than rectangular, a bit like a tennis court surrounded by football fans, but the proximity of the crowd to the pitch makes for a terrific atmosphere. I believe they actually moved the kick-off back a few minutes to allow as many of us as possible us to get in before the football began. The visiting fans took particular delight in mocking short-arse John Spencer, who must have hated the trend for long shorts, which allowed him barely a kneecapful of flesh on display. He made SuperKev look like a giant, and he trudged miserably to take each corner in front of us to a chorus of "hi ho, hi ho, it's off to work we go!"

This being a couple of months after the Nightmare at Elm Park which had prompted Reidy to change personnel, we were on a bit of a roll. Perez was now protected by the youthful defence of Darren Holloway, Mickey Gray, Jody Craddock and Darren Williams. Mad Alex Rae won the ball, gave it to Lee Clark, and he gave it to Summerbee or Johnston. Buzza and Magic then fed Quinn and Phillips, simple and effective. The home side's central defenders decided that the only way to handle Quinny was to kick lumps out of him, but he still spent a large portion of the game making them look silly. In a lop-sided first half he hit the woodwork twice and had one disallowed, presumably for being too skilful. The big fella was having an absolute field day, and they just couldn't deal with him, but we were beginning to think that the vital breakthrough would never come. When it did, it was one of those special goals that seemed to occur in slow motion. As the game entered the final minutes, a left-wing cross floated over Steve Morrow's head and dropped onto Niall's right boot. 4000 Sunderland voices screamed, "hit it!" but the big man had other ideas. He waited until Morrow turned to face him, dummied the ball past him, and blasted a left foot rocket into the top corner, right in front of us. Ecstasy on the terraces, of the emotional variety, and I scared the fat bloke in front of me by planting a kiss right on top of his baldy heed. "You'll not see nothing like the mighty Quinn" boomed across West London well beyond the final whistle, and we poured out of the ground in a mighty good mood. We haven't lost there since, so the boys on the field that day broke a very big jinx and knocked QPR off our lengthy list of bogey teams.

The game had provided enough good memories to keep us happy on the homeward journey, but we weren't finished yet. Our landlord pal had managed to blag a bunch of passes into the players' lounge. Sadly, this option became unavailable soon after, due to his contact becoming a little too attached to some of the fixtures and fittings of said players' lounge. By the time the players began to arrive, some greedy buggers had eaten most of the buffet and were standing sheepishly at the bar. First in was Lionel, who swept past us like a gladiator twice the size of Russell Crowe – I'd never seen a goalie that big without being fat. As one, our merry band shouted "hey Lionel, comment ça va?" Realising immediately that we had reached the limit of our linguistic flexibility, he shrugged his massive shoulders as only a Frenchman could, and beat a hasty path to the bar. We chatted with all of our players apart from Lee ClarkIdiot, who was on the treatment table getting his ankle sorted, and Quinny, who was so busy talking to the press that a tannoy announcement had to be made to get him onto the team bus before it left. Niall Quinn talking too much?

Who would have believed it? We did our amateur interview with Buzza, along the lines of, "Nicky, why did you leave City?" Answer, "It was time for a change", and were surprised to find that Gareth Hall had escaped from his loan to Brentford to appear as a thankfully unused sub, and was threatening to take Nicky on a tour of the West End nightspots that he wasn't yet barred out of.

As Steve Morrow and his partner in thuggery Karl Ready finally entered, we shouted "watch yer ankles, lads", and hopped around clutching our shins as they passed. They didn't know which way to look, and were further embarrassed when we pushed past them to get an autograph from Cedric off TFI Friday.

As time drew on, it became obvious that we'd need a taxi to get to King's Cross on time, so I headed for the phone, pushing past some bloke blocking the corridor. If you listened to Five Live that night, you may well have heard Ray Harford's interview interrupted by a thump and my cry of "watch yer back, scholar!" As we sat outside awaiting our cab, a vaguely familiar figure, in the regulation ex-pro's demob suit of beige mac with upturned collar, brushed past, and a voice called out "Stan Bowles; one of the finest footballers to grace the green fields of the English game in the seventies." He was politeness itself, saying that we'd go up and that we'd spend big (which we didn't and didn't), before disappearing into the night. No sign of the taxi at the promised time, so several more phone calls were made before we discovered the cabbie in question sitting half asleep in an unmarked Volvo about ten yards away.

He did get us to the station in time to collect swag, scran, and Sobs's luggage. We enjoyed a couple of cans and a SAFC picture quiz before disembarking at Darlo and hitting the Number Twenty2 pub, where our three bags and a huge suitcase were really popular on a busy Saturday night. Sobs, who had countered jet lag all day by using the time-honoured remedy of alcohol, finally succumbed on the last leg of the journey, resulting in a bag being left on the bus. We were a perfect sight as we arrived, giggling, at chez Sobs, either side of the largest surviving item of luggage, all that was keeping us upright. A series of frantic phone calls to GNER, the Number Twenty2, Station Taxis, and GoAhead Northern finally resulted in the missing bag being recovered on Monday evening, complete with duty free, presents, and passport. Normal relations with the family resumed soon after.

R

Rotherham

Like Barnsley, Rotherham is just an optimistic couple of hours down the road from Wearside, and has generally been good to us results-wise. We only played them for the first time in 1958 when we had dropped a division a couple of years earlier and they had come up. At Millmoor, Kichenbrand, with a hat-trick, and Revie scored as we made up for a goal-free first half and won 4-1. Perhaps the only game in which two players called Don have scored for us. They held us at Roker, and even did the double over us the following season, but for the next few seasons we won four and drew three of the eight games. After 1964, thanks to us getting promoted and relegated about a dozen times, and Rotherham just getting relegated, we had seventeen years apart. In the early eighties we beat them in the League and FA Cup, then we were back in the same division after we forgot to get promoted after a relegation and dropped to the Third. They must have hated us, as not only did we win 4-1 at their place at the end of the season, but hit them for seven at our place in the Sherpa Vans Trophy, with Keith Berstschin getting two, and only a month later watched Gatesy score all three without reply. After that, it was another ten years to the FA Cup tie in January 1998.

TallPaul had been desperate to give Rotherham a try for some reason, so we hopped on the Durham Bus and headed down the A1. Rather than head into town, as we'd heard it was a bit scruffy, we decided just to walk up the road from the ground and try that. We duly wandered up to the junction, looked to our left and didn't see anything that resembled a pub, and therefore turned right. There were several places that passed for pubs, but we picked what the landlord happily described as the roughest pub in town. Who were we to argue, so we popped our ten pence in the pool table and set about enjoying ourselves. While the beer was strictly of "matchday only" quality, it was remarkably cheap, and thankfully there were none of the locals who made the place so rough in that day. In fact, I don't remember a pub in the proximity of a football ground being so quiet on a matchday. Apart from ourselves, there were two miserable looking old lads at the bar, smoking Woodbines, seeing who could pull their flat cap the closest to their eyes, and not uttering a word for the whole of our stay. After our fourth game, a lad of about twelve wandered in carrying a pool cue in a case, and dropped his ten pence on the edge of the table. Ah, we thought, the local hustler trying to win some money for sweets. Cool as you like, he popped another ten pence in the machine on the wall that dispensed mints in a plastic container in the shape of a crocodile, and waited for the end of our game. "On you go son" said TallPaul, and the youth racked them up like a pro. He chalked his cue and proceeded to produce a display of such hopeless ineptitude that we wondered if he understood any of the rules, never mind how to hold a cue and strike a ball. After the first game, it became apparent that this was the best that he could do, and that he couldn't hustle a smile from his grandma, so we tried to let him pot a few by leaving one of his colours over the pocket. All to no avail, and I suspect that if we'd waited until he won a game, not only would we have missed the football, but we'd have been to his wedding and been made godparents to his first two children as well.

Filled with cheap beer and dreams of Wembley, we hit Millmoor (though not very hard, otherwise it would have fallen down) and followed our ticket instructions to the Railway End I believe it was called. If you ever feel like criticising your home-town, take a look at Rotherham, which has had no money whatsoever spent on it since 1952. From the varied collection of scrap yards to the very disused cabin cruiser parked on the railway line next to the away end, this is an open-air museum of industrial decay. The walls bore signs which read "walk slowly and carefully" – presumably so that the "guard dogs on patrol" could catch you.

The alley down the side of the stand was barely wide enough for a car to pass through, and yet that was where the buses parked, meaning that the first one in was naturally the last one out. It was packed solid with Sunderland fans marvelling at the number of scrap yards on the left, and the rickety state of the stand to the right. The old lad on the turnstile had obviously never seen so many visitors in many a year, and he managed to keep my part of the ticket and give me the stub back. The lights hanging from the roof were like those you used to see in hospitals, just the one bulb on a long wire, in a wide conical shade, and only about half of them worked. The South Yorkshire annex of the Museum of Football Stadia through the ages, Millmoor followed the Watford theme with a selection of hotch-potch constructions randomly arranged around a piece of grass, although it has to be said that it was a nice piece of grass. They put seats in the Railway end a few years ago, and fisticuffs almost ensued when I was accused of pushing my seat into the legs of the bloke behind me. He obviously hadn't noticed that there was only a foot or so between the front of his seat and the back of mine – it was terraces with seats rather than part of the ground designed to accommodate seats. They also got themselves a mascot, Dusty Dumpling, who must be the cheapest mascot in the professional game. Maybe his Mam made the costume when she'd had a drink or two, but I hope they kept him on when they moved to the Don Valley Stadium on the other side of the M1 – Sheffield.

To say it was overcrowded was understating it a bit, as 11,5000 must have been about capacity, and those travellers lucky enough to have tickets at the end of the side (if that makes sense) had a good laugh as those of us in the end swayed about uncontrollably – if one of us moved, we all moved. Anyway, we were up for the Cup on the back of what had become a barnstorming season. We were massive favourites to win it (the game, not the Cup), as we were very much the Big Boys from up the road, and Rotherham were very much the Minnows on this occasion. We had our settled defence of Lionel, Holloway, Mickey Gray, Craddock, and Darren Williams. We had our settled midfield of Clark, Rae, Summerbee, and Johnson, and we had the forward line that was the envy of every team in the land – Quinn and Phillips.

For the first forty five minutes, it was a case of Rotherham playing like demons and us taking a lot of decent attacking play by them in our stride, but Phillips tucked away a penalty at the far end to settle our nerves. Our one goal lead at the break made us hope that the Millers would run out of steam in the second half. As the players were no doubt being sworn at by Reidy and Saxton, we attempted to go to the toilet, but you only went if everybody around you wanted to go as well. Let's just say that the tide was well and truly in when we got there, and a lot of tiptoeing ensued. Ten minutes into the second half, and little Kev was there again, right in front of us, to raise our spirits. Ten minutes after that, Garner, who'd been the energetic heart of most of Rotherham's football, scored on the break, and it was a nervous couple of minutes until we realised that they were knackered. SKP scored twice in five minutes, Mad Alex terrorised their midfield, and that Clark popped the ball out wide to Buzza and Magic. Quinny netted the fifth with five left, and TallPaul reckoned that we could have doubled our score if we'd really put our minds to it. 5-1 against anybody, especially away from home, and with your main man getting four, is a result that we were very happy with.

As we celebrated, the home fans breathed a sigh of relief that it was all over, with a brave performance, but class telling in the end. That was the good bit over, now it was time to try to get out. The WPC by the gate tried her best to keep the exiting throng moving to where she wanted them to go, but some needed to piddle again, and her partner whispered something in her ear which must have gone along the lines of "I'd just let them leave of their own accord if I were you. There's nowhere they can go but into that alley." So we sort of flowed out of Millmoor, swept left, and surged along the alley, past the scrap yards and back to the buses with many of the shorter members of the Red and White Army managing it without their feet touching the ground. Having got stuck at the wrong side of the alley, we were three buses past ours before we managed to work our way over to the other side and go against the flow to climb aboard.

Back on the bus for first in, last out, wait for the crowd to thin out enough for us to move without killing a few dozen, and a couple of uneventful hours later we were back home and planning the next phase of our FA Cup watching campaign.

 is for Scunthorpe

I know that the game in July 2007 was not a league game, but it was an enjoyable and eventful trip wrapped around a poor game, so it fits the criteria for this list of tales perfectly.

The day started interestingly enough as I headed for Bishop Station, as a cavalcade of 1940s vehicles rumbled down Newgate Street – off to help the victims of the latest flood, which put the day's journey in both doubt and perspective – and I took on board one of the Red Star Café's cholesterol specials, just in case I forgot to eat anything later on. Age might bring wisdom, but it doesn't entirely do away with football-related daftness, so it's wise to think ahead before getting carried away when the football kicks in. While Darlo a few days earlier had technically been an away game, the amount of folks in work attire showed that it was a bit of a doozy in terms of effort – closer than Sunderland for many - but Scunny was a proper away game, the real deal, which is necessary for the likes of myself, who managed to bugger up the train arrangements. This meant that by the time Heather rang to inform me of an empty seat next to her and Al, they were at Donny and I was just boarding at Darlo. I'd told them that I'd be on the 9:30, they'd thought I meant Durham when I'd meant Bishop, so they were heading south while I was still wondering why they didn't do black pudding in the Red Star Café.

Thankfully, there's always someone you know on a train on the way to a Sunderland game. As I passed Paul Mulley for the fourth time looking for carriage B, he explained that we were on it. That was just before Heather's phone call. Ah well, Paul and I go back years as far as Sunderland are concerned, so there was a chance to chew the fat over events long gone and events unfolding at SR5 at that time. When we got to Donny, where I'd been due to meet up with the Birtley

Two for a quick tour of the local alehouses, there was some sort of security alert on platform one, which wasn't much of a surprise as there were numerous dodgy characters about. Well, I was on my own, they weren't in SAFC colours and this looked decidedly dodgy – or maybe I'm just being paranoid – but I didn't see whatever it was causing the alert as various folks rushed around with their high-vis jackets, walkie-talkies, and nervous expressions. When the Cleethorpes train arrived, the guard with the world's biggest twitch confirmed that it was for Scunthorpe and thus the one for me, so off I went on what must be one of the most depressing train journeys in the world. They still have grey pit-heaps and pit-head gear, for goodness sake, among the rest of the industrial dereliction. They could open a film studio there, and film all the futuristic post-apocalyptic, underground human freedom fighters against the robot or alien rulers of the world, that sort of thing. I seem to remember this part of the world – the Isle of Axholme - being touted as a famous market garden area, but the allotments on view from the train were largely filled with scrap cars. Some thirty years ago, my university room-mate Mick from Donny had written his dissertation on the agricultural diversity of the Isle of Axeholme, and having now seen the place I must put his opus magna forward for every literary prize there is. Fiction and fantasy, obviously.

My eyes dulled by the flat landscape and my brain likewise from the aforementioned industrial wasteland, I eventually disembarked at Scunthorpe station. As it's about a mile east of the new ground, I'd told my would-be drinking companions for the day that I'd meet them in the pub just down the road towards the town. I eventually met up with Al 'n Heff in the Honest Lawyer as planned, chatting away to a lad I knew from various away games over the years, and who, it transpired, had grown up just round the corner from them and had gone to school with Al's brother. The pub was smashing beer-wise, but the scran included things like "a chiffonade of leaves" (lettuce, I think) and other such nonsense, which was surprising when you consider that the landlord was from Aycliffe. So we nipped down to the 'Spoons, one of that chain of pubs which has, in recent years, become a bit of a lifesaver for the travelling football fan. I realise that they can be much of a muchness, and in some of them you could be forgiven for not knowing if you were in Aberdeen or Penzance, but they're cheap, they all sell proper beer (usually in good condition) and do food at every conceivable hour of the day. Or so it seems. Things quickly took a bad turn as the Polis outside was heard to say "ah've been black and white aal me life like, me." Inside were the usual youngsters trying their first pint at an away game – had I been on the bar, I would have asked their dad for I.D., and the usual smattering of local ruffians out to pick a fight with the fans of the visiting so-called big team. With our safety in mind, we wolfed down our beer and burger special and shot back to the Lawyer for more decent beer and a double Dekka – two shots of whatever Irish Whiskey takes your fancy – as we took our first chance that season, football-wise, to raise a glass to Pos on the fifth anniversary of his passing.

Absent friends...

As we'd done the usual and taken our eye off the ball timewise, we needed a quick taxi to the ground, and there it was – a new stadium, in the now traditional retail park location, with a depressing number of pillars to obscure your view. A little bit different from the rest of the flatpack grounds in that respect, and a chance to bob and weave to keep the ball in view. Almost a year into his tenure, Roy Keane had put out a bit of an unusual team, with no natural wide-men in the starting eleven, no sign of would-be hard-man-cum-midfield general Graham Kavanagh, and a first appearance for "don't mess with" Etuhu. We'd barely worked out who the players were when what looked like a blatant hand-ball let Scunny in and their lad calmly passed the ball into the net. That was only two minutes or so into the game, and therefore qualifies as not the best of starts. For the second consecutive game in a few days, I was paired in the seats with Mad Gerrard McClurey, and we, along with the others, tried our best to get the team going by the time-honoured method of shouting, screaming, and singing like idiots. Unfortunately, there was no natural shape on the field. Dwight Yorke tried a swerver which didn't swerve as we tried to press, but Scunny were always first to the ball in midfield and thus were able to keep the pressure on. On the half hour, Darren Ward showed his worth with a fine save off his legs, and the rebound was put wastefully (from a Scunny point of view) way over the top. We had a decent penalty shout just before the break after one of a number of wild tackles from the home side but nothing was given.

Half-time was a bit like being thirteen again – down to the bikeshed and spot all the lads having a crafty smoke. You could have seen the fug back in Sunderland.

The second half saw the expected plethora of substitutions that go with pre-season friendlies, with Stern John and David Connolly going up front and Liam Miller replacing Super Dick Etuhu. There was also some bloke we didn't recognise appearing in the middle of defence but was apparently a trialist called Jack Pelter from New Zealand. He managed exactly no first team appearances in his year with us, played the same number for Valerenga, then was back down under to Waitakere. We also had Billy Dennehy making a rare start for the first team.

Actually, he only ever played for our reserves and in friendlies before seven loan appearances for the mighty Accrington Stanley and then a trip back across the Irish Sea to Derry, Cork, and Shamrock Rovers. If there'd been a reserve league the previous year, more folk would have recognised him, and as it was the lad tried very hard but to no avail. As the game wore on, we accepted that we were going to get nothing from the ref, and that Scunny are a more than decent side who would probably do quite well in the Championship in the coming season, and that we were a bit off colour and out of shape. Murphy's late effort that shaved the post almost got us something we barely deserved, and then it was all over.

Of Keane's summer signings, Chopra had little to feed off due to our strange shape - let's call it experimental, as that's what pre-season is partly about - and Etuhu was probably crowded out for the same reasons, so it was difficult to make realistic judgements on the new lads, including the mystery man at the back, Jack Pelter, as you now know. He had a name that sounded perfect for the Northern League, and to be fair, that was probably his level in the English game. Stern John had continued where he'd left off in the Darlington match on the Wednesday, as if he'd never met his team-mates before, while Connolly, in contrast, looked sharp.

There was a bunch of youth giving the team grief at the end, screaming – "don't you f*****g come and clap me, you useless b*****ds" who were probably the same ones acting as if we'd won the FA Cup when we had strolled past a pretty poor Darlo side on Wednesday. Hell man, it was only a friendly, that's the kind of mentality that should be the preserve of the "not fit to wear the shirt" Man Utd fans who smash the house up every time they don't win the treble. It was a friendly, it was a try-out formation, it was disjointed, it went wrong – so there were a few hours left to make a decent day of it. Shit happens at every team and you should know that it's part of football. It wouldn't be much fun without it.
Outside the ground, there were free buses on to take us to the station, which was nice. Until the station turned out to be Althorpe, which was one barn, a small housing estate in the middle of nowhere, and a busload of Sunderland fans who most certainly did not want to be there. It was not where we wanted to be. Smart-arse PC 171 guaranteed that, despite what was printed on my ticket, the next train would take me to Donny. I had people to meet at Scunthorpe Station – what if I'd had their tickets? A letter of complaint winged its way to the local Chief Constable soon after that one. I reckoned at the time that the police state we were heading for under Thatcher was still just waiting under the surface and the longer we let them get away with stunts like that, the more likely it was

to re-appear. I was vexed, to say the least, at this removal of our civil liberties, and I haven't changed my opinion since.

As it happened, it was the only train that went to Althorpe, which made the decision to send it there in the first place all the more puzzling. Talk about making a rod for their own backs.

So we managed an unplanned hour in Donny, where we did what we'd planned to do at eleven that morning – have a few beers. We tried the Plough, which had turned us away on our way to Sheff Wed the previous season because Donny were playing Scunny, and we were football fans and thus likely to cause trouble. The beer was excellent but the bogs stunk like you wouldn't believe, and the Tut, which was a bit scary when Hey Jude came on the jukebox and a bloke tried very obviously to get off with Al (believe me, if I were that way inclined I wouldn't try it on with Al - no offence, mate) and me (believe me, if I were that way inclined I would), so we were on the train four minutes earlier than planned. Being a rebel, I broke the rules on my train ticket and stayed on until Durham instead of Darlo – call it recompense for the Althorpe incident - and rounded the night off with a spot of traditional Mag-baiting in the Half Moon. Steve is a nice lad and good barman, but he's a Mag, and therefore a target that was fired at on every possible occasion.

Sheffield Utd

Back in September 2004, we'd won at Elland Road thanks to a goal from Carl Robinson, a decent-ish player, but not one who will live long in the memories of most Sunderland fans. Not for lack of effort on the lad's part, he was a willing and brave enough competitor, but firmly in the journeyman mould. After that win, we decided that we had reaped what we had sown and our midfield squad was both versatile and effective with players being interchangeable and adaptable. Four days later, we had the chance to see just how adaptable and versatile they were, or not, as we played the same starting eleven – so every chance of another win on the road.

As we gathered at Thinford, we cast a curse and wished a pox on the fixture computer operators – may the fleas of a thousand camels infest their collective crotch, and may their arms be too short to scratch it (Old Bishop Curse #46b). Yet another midweek away game meant yet more time off work, and a flying pick up at Aycliffe meant that the living sculpture (fruit remains and Sunderland favours, involving a 'nana skin, peach stone, gowk, and George's cap) would remain unfinished atop the wall to the rear of Thinford Saddlery. Viewings are still free (naturally), and the development of this symbiotic representation of post-industrial county Durham and its interface with its football club of choice reflects to this day the hopes and fears of a generation. On the other hand, George took his cap away, the vegetable matter was eaten by birds and rodents, and there was nothing but a small stain there next time we looked. One of the benefits of boarding the bus at Thinford was that it was (still is, of course) on the A167, the natural habitat of the Ferryhill Roman. He marches from Ferryhill north along the old Great North Road to Thinford and beyond, then turns round and marches back again. It lightens the mood and adds a bit of interest while you wait for your bus to see him in whichever fighting uniform of ancient times he chooses – he does Spartans as well – marching past oblivious to the attention he attracts. Why does he do it? Because he likes it, simple as that. Good luck to the man.

The outward journey was a tale of folks getting their names down for the Monday of tatie-picking week game at Rotherham, having secured the last half-day holiday available to them, or, in one case, admitting defeat and missing their first game in nearly five years. They should think about this sort of thing when Sky comes a-knocking, because it does really upset us when we can't get to the game, and they vent their spleen on those fortunate to have attended when next they see a match. The second half of the journey was largely taken up with trying to stem the flow of blood from a shaving cut (some folks like to look smart at the game, heaven knows why), and leaving the poor lad smelling of "Angel" perfume – we draw the line at taking emergency aftershave on the bus, even in these days of metro-sexuality - and with half a newspaper on his face. When he decided that his face had healed sufficiently for the paper to be removed, it left the word "sex" backwards on his face. Nothing like standing out in a crowd.

As it was Sheffield, we made plans to stop off at Doncaster, as it was less than half an hour away. Every day is market day in Doncaster, apparently, so it was to a busy Wetherspoons that we retired - rather an apt word, as our busload represented the only customers, amongst over a hundred, in gainful employment. We were the only ones who'd had a shave or bought any clothes in the last five years as well, but we'll leave that. As the staff didn't seem inclined to invoke the Wetherspoon rule of no card games for cash, we ploughed on with the usual ten bob a game Rachel. Lee "Maverick" was up to his usual card tricks, that of winning without understanding how, and thus prompting one of us to quote Omar Sharif from Channel 4 poker - "yee've been looking at my effing cards." If there's one thing you can say about Donny, it's that you stood no chance of being refused entry to a pub because of the way you dress. The staff were far too worried about which of the locals was about to either thump his (or her, the lasses didn't look that fussy) drinking companions. We decided that we should try a real pub, one frequented by non-alcoholics, so we wandered across the market place, me picking up a replacement flat cap for only three quid in the process. The Queens was the nearest option, but as there was a full-on disco taking place and the pavement outside was scattered with semi-conscious party-goers and broken glass, we came to the conclusion that it wasn't for us. Thankfully, we found a secret boozer with lots of little rooms, nice beer, and even nicer sandwiches. That did us nicely until it was time to leave.

Being sensible sorts, we always arrive at the ground in time to break the promise that we make at the start of every season – the one about not bothering to drink the rubbish beer on or nearby the ground for the hour or so we usually have to spare. Luckily, the Polis outside the Cricketers would not believe we were from Donny (wrong accents) or Scunny (not wearing slippers) and denied us entry "for our own safety". The Cricketers, for those of you who are interested, was right outside the away end, and was at one time run by none other than Big Bad Billy Whitehurst. I doubt if he'd have let any untoward behaviour take place. Mr Winks had snuck in, probably because his neighbour Carl Robinson had left word during his recent loan spell there that any friend of his should be allowed a pint. As we were his eighth club, the Cricketers probably made a canny living on his neighbours popping in for a pint. Inside Bramall Lane, and it was obvious that our end had yet to benefit from any redevelopment, remaining smoky, smelly, steep, and largely made of red-painted wood. At least the Clock-Stand style seats had been big and comfy enough, and, unlike their plastic descendants, retain body heat and so prevent haemorrhoids. Well done the Sheffield Health Authority.

On the field, we sank to the level of an opposition team with as much football in them as a broken window. Even Paul Thirlwell, United captain for the night in honour of his sparkling Wearside career, seemed bemused by their tactics of "kick it as hard and as far as you can in any direction", but not as bemused as us. Add to that a baffling double dismissal which included Gary Breen and future Sunderland no-scoring forward Andy Gray, for violent conduct – by Gary Breen? Give over! It had looked for all the world like no more than a bit of parallel jogging, and the game as a spectacle fell to pieces.

The eleven players who had looked so comfortable, flexible, and effective against Leeds a few days earlier looked as uncomfortable and inflexible as it was possible for eleven so-called team-mates to look. Poom, Stephen Wright, McCartney, Breen, Caldwell, Carter, Whitley, Robinson, Whitehead, Chris Brown, and Stephen Elliott – none of them enjoyed much of a night, with only the keeper producing anything positive of note. We created nothing of any quality, and were crying out for someone to put their foot on the ball, look up, and play a decent pass. Maybe Hoolio could well have made all the difference. As it was, it looked like 0-0 with one up front each after defender (it says defender on his CV, so he must be a defender) Mark Lynch replaced Brown, until Whitley's header evaded Caldwell, and then it looked 0-1. The other two subs, lightweights John Oster and loanee Simon Johnson, could unsurprisingly make no difference and it was a miserable two hours home. At least Sheffield is close enough to get back in time to dissect the game on TV – if you're that way inclined.

Shrewsbury

Our trip to Gay Meadow, one of the more colourfully named grounds in the land, came too soon, or too late, depending on your outlook. Bob Stokoe had returned in an ultimately unsuccessful bid to clear up the mess that Mackemenemy had left us in back in 1987, and we had but a handful of games left in which to preserve our Second Division status. I know it sounds awful, but it really did happen. In the 21st century, of course, such a blow would be softened by the fact that it would only be a drop to League One, but even clever marketing like that couldn't hide the pain of probable relegation from true fans.

Being the end of season, we managed to pull in the usual detritus of West Ham fans exiled in Bish (Pop), and got B&B arranged on the outskirts of Shrewsbury. We duly parked up at the White Swan, frightened the landlord by tossing a tenner apiece into an ashtray and calling it "kitty." I know a tenner sounds like barely enough for a round of drinks, but back then it was a night out for four. We strolled the mile or so to the town centre, a list of potential watering holes written on a hand-drawn map. We'd arranged to meet Reg, up from Ipswich, in the Castle Vaults, as it served Marston's beers and Mexican scran, and we were on holiday and fancied a bit of culture. The landlord had other ideas – the Smoggies had been there the week before and made a bit of a mess, so we weren't allowed in. Buggers. The Teddy Boy on the door at the Station Hotel asked how many of us there were, "Four? I can handle that", so that was us settled for our pre-match drink.

A lovely sunny day saw the Red and White Army basking on the terraces at Gay Meadow, shirts off. Our pre kick-off performance even prompted the local constabulary to ask what we did when we won a game. It brought the usual response from his colleague of "don't be daft; they've only been following them for 30 years". As we'd won five of our six matches against the Shrews, the only slip-up being earlier in the season with a draw at Roker, we expected a win in the sunshine.The best fun of the afternoon was the little old gadgie running around three sides of the ground every time the ball went over the stand into the Severn. Thanks to the antics of our Teesside pals the previous week, they having sunk the coracle, he had to carry a net on a ten foot pole to retrieve the ball, and drew huge applause from the away end as he hobbled past. In a typical end of season battle, Benno diverted Mark Proctor's shot in to the net for the only goal, and we left the ground convinced that salvation was guaranteed.

Back into the Station, where we knocked back a couple of celebratory pints before the local nutter arrived, in a temper so obviously foul that we put it down to the home team losing. Unsurprisingly, it was my turn to fetch the beers, so, as he stood at the bar cursing and swearing at everything that moved, I sidled up next to him. "Four pints of best?" I asked, in my best middle England accent. He caught me by the eye immediately. "Been to the match?" he snarled. No point hiding the fact, I thought, so I replied "aye". It then turned out that the reason for his foul temper was that he'd backed Alex Higgins to win the snooker, and he'd fallen over drunk, as he was wont to do, and cost our new mate a tenner. We enjoyed an hour or so with him, re-living Shrewsbury's greatest moments (how did we stretch it to 60 minutes?) before setting out on the pub crawl to end most pub crawls. We fell in with a Sunderland fan who was Hereford born and bred, and had apparently taken to us after our joyous response to the Mags' hilarious FA Cup exit in his home town. He knew where most of the pubs were on our list, which was just as well, as the map had long since been used for something unmentionable. We ended up back at our White Swan just in time to get a double round of Pedigree in, and watch Dave "boy" Macauley knock seven bells out of some poor contender in the boxing ring. Sharing our accommodation was an American, christened "Okie from Muskokie" by John, due to the daft bugger's fondness for repeatedly stating the bloody obvious. It turned out he was on a grand tour of Europe. A grand tour which he'd be lucky to survive, if his habit of talking over everybody else in the room, and failing to understand anything that wasn't American, persisted on the continent.

Breakfast came in the form of a pint left on the window sill from the night before, then the full English job. Oh, and the Weetabix. Have you ever seen a man eat Weetabix without milk? Under normal circumstances, it's bad enough, but after a gutful of Shropshire's finest ale the night before, Pop's antics at the breakfast table had to be seen to be believed. Our American friend (?) made one snide comment too many ("is he talking to God on the big white telephone"), prompting the normally restrained John to threaten him with the insertion of a buttered toast rack.

The Sunday morning was a sunny delight, which we enjoyed in the Riverside Park with the second issue of the Sunday Sport. A man who turns into a leopard? That's when we decided it wasn't worth taking seriously. A quick trip up the M6, and we were in Lymm for our lunchtime bevy. The fact that Denis Tueart lived there had no influence on our decision to stop off there, and he never showed up for the domino handicap in the Spread Eagle anyway. A couple of beers later, and John's sensible motoring ensured that we were back in Bish with plenty of time for a Sunday night of celebration. At least we didn't know what was to happen at the end of the season (you big bugger, Cascarino, you pretend Irishman, you), and were able to enjoy the moment. You have to do that following Sunderland, as looking too far ahead can be injurious to your health.

S is also for Stoke

I t will be no surprise that not much ever happens in Stoke itself, because it doesn't have a town centre to speak of – as I found when I left my sister to look at the shops while I went to the match. She had a great time sitting in the car all afternoon. My wife's lasting impression of the place is from April '81, at the nearest motorway junction, where the Pink Panther and Andy Pandy, complete with red and white scarves, were hitching a lift after the match. She wanted me to give them a lift, but as I only had two seats, and we were sitting in them, the fancily dressed Mackems had to be left to their own devices.

Back in February '76, I set out for the 5th round FA Cup-tie at Stoke, taking up my usual position at the south end of the Tyne Bridge, with my thumb out and my scarf safely hidden from view. Self preservation was something that came naturally after living in bandit country for the previous five months. It didn't take long for a car to stop, but my heart sank when I saw the occupants – four lads in Mag colours. I opened my coat so that the driver could see my scarf, expecting a two-fingered salute followed by the screeching of tyres as they left. On the contrary, they shrugged their shoulders and invited me aboard. They looked reasonable lads, for Mags, so I accepted their kind offer. Brave, I know, as they could well have eaten me at any time.

Their views on my choice of team were predictable, and somewhat familiar. "A Sunderland supporter at university? Don't believe you". They even had a friend who would not acknowledge that Sunderland existed as a place. Nothing has changed, has it?

They were on their way to Bolton for the FA Cup match, you know, the one where Supawhiskymac scored over his shoulder, so they agreed to drop me at the

Hartshead services on the M62 to try for a connecting lift to the Potteries. I was allowed to share their bait, and even got two cans of Brown given. Surely these were not true Mags? Was the pease pudding poisoned? Was the Brown laced with arsenic? I ate and drank nervously, as we chatted about our footballing experiences until we reached Hartshead, where reality kicked in. I got a few funny looks as I climbed (red and white) out of their car (black and white), and, as we said our farewells and I checked my coat pockets for booby-traps, we saw the reason why. The place was like the Bigg Market on a Friday night, as a mixture of Sunderland and Skunk fans expressed their mutual dislike in the most physical of manners.

I dodged the more expressive discussions, and got into the safe (truck drivers') part of the café, where I secured a lift to Stoke on a minibus from Hylton Red House. An hour of drinking on the move, then the driver got lost as soon as we left the M6. We spent what seemed like an hour driving aimlessly through the houses near the ground, complaining about the local accent being hard to understand when we asked for directions. By the time we got parked up, there was no time to nip for a beer, which was just as well, as I've never yet found anywhere at all near the Victoria Ground, or its replacement, worth going near. Over 41,000 were at the Victoria Ground to see the lads achieve exactly what they set out to do – frustrate the home side to bits with a dour 0-0 and take them back to 47,500 at Roker. We were doing the business in the league as we homed in on eventual promotion, so a chance to play a First Division side in the FA Cup was a good test of our credentials. As he would in the away game early the next season, Bob Stokoe played Jackie Ashurst, Moncur, and Jeff Clarke as central defenders in front of Bolton and Malone, and it worked. Towers, Kerr, and Tom Finney (no, not that Tom Finney) worked hard in front of them, while Pop and Mel were afforded few chances up front. Great result, though, and in the replay, Pop and Mel repeated their third round performance with a goal each to earn us a quarter-final at home to Palace. A pox on Alan Whittle and bloody stupid felt hats.

After the match came the tricky bit. Getting home. It may be cheap to travel by thumb, but it can be unreliable, especially when the roads are very busy just after a match. Luckily, I chanced on some mates travelling on the Aclet bus, and was offered the use of an empty seat for about 60 pence. An evening in Sheffield had been planned, so we sang our way across the Pennines to the Steel City. Our first port of call was the lounge of a pub near Bramall Lane, where the pairs of pensioners were treated to our singing the current favourite of the club singers, "Bohemian Rhapsody", along with the jukebox. We tried as many of the town centre pubs as we could, and I impressed the lads by signing them into the Students' Union bar, where they were impressed with the price, but not the taste, of their first pint of Ward's. 11:30 departure, and back in Bishop by about five hours too late for the last bus back to Tyneside. So it was a quiet scramble in through my Mam's lavvy window, and a note on the kitchen table telling her there would be one more for breakfast that Sunday. Happy Days.

Station

Subway For ⚏ Seven Sisters Station
pass through the subway
to Exit 4, and follow signs

SEVEN SISTERS STATION

MIKE DOCHERTY
SUNDERLAND

ottenham Hotspur – Spurs As it can be both an S and a T, or even an H if I'd been really stuck, it leads nicely from one to the other.

1977 wasn't much of a year for Sunderland, and is chiefly remembered for the intervention of a certain bearded person in the season's denouement. I'd have included the word "allegedly", but then that might prevent him taking legal action, and I'd welcome the chance to have my day in court discussing his alleged non-involvement on that and at least one other occasion that has proved damaging to my beloved Sunderland Football Club. Anyway, by the time we played at White Hart Lane in April of that year, we were well and truly up to our red and white necks in the sticky brown stuff. The purple patch of February, with the emergence of the Wearside Trinity of Elliott, Arnott, and Rowell, and all of those goals, had settled down to a fairly decent run of form in which we'd only lost twice in eleven games, and there was the hint of a little light at the end of the tunnel. Having drawn at Leeds and beaten Man Utd at home, there was no way I was going to miss a game at Spurs with the chance of more points in the salvation pot.

Being still young and daft, as opposed to old and daft, I suggested to my girlfriend that it would be a good idea to visit her folks in Bristol. Suggestion accepted, we hitched down on the Friday and got to Keynsham, which was close enough to Bristol to warrant a phone call to her dad to come and pick us up. Being a friendly sort, he was good enough to give me a lift the next morning to the motorway so that I could take the cheapskate route to the capital. If you are at all familiar with the layout of motorways around Bristol you'll know that the M32 out of town joins the M4 at a roundabout – at the time, I believe it was the only all-motorway roundabout in the country. Naturally, as it was a roundabout, I assumed it was allowed to use it for hitchhiking purposes. Not so. Ten minutes of thumbing had passed when Avon's finest rolled up in the latest Ford Zodiac, and informed me that I was a pedestrian trespassing on a motorway, and asked why I was there. I thought the Sunderland scarf and the outstretched arm, complete with extended thumb, would have given the game away, but no. I had to explain that I was trying to get from my girlfriend's house in Bristol to Spurs to see Sunderland play. They even asked to see a photo of her, which, being a soppy sort, I had in my wallet. "Should have stayed at home, son" was all they could come up with before issuing me with a fixed penalty of £10, which was a fair amount in those days. They didn't even offer me a lift to a place at which it was legal to hitchhike, and if you are at all familiar with the layout of motorways around Bristol, you'll know that there's no way to get away from that roundabout on foot without recourse to yomping several miles across the fields, no doubt to a chorus of "get orf moi laaahhnd!" and a volley of shotgun fire. I'm not sure where they expected me to go, so I wandered away, hid in the bushes for what a considered enough time for the law to be pestering someone else a few miles away, then got the thumb back out.

Luckily, the Great British Public are much more accommodating than the police when it comes to getting poor students from A to B when all they have to get them there is their thumb. One lift later, I was at the end of the Chiswick Flyover, that monument to sixties transport planning and civil engineering, the traditional eastern end of the thumber's route between London and the West Country. How to get to Spurs, though? It might say London on Tottenham Hotspur Football Club's address, but Tottenham is about as close to Chiswick as Bishop is to Sunderland. Well, that's what the tube was built for, wasn't it? To get football fans from their arrival point in London to whichever ground they desired? Into Chiswick Park tube station and an hour or so later, I arrived at Seven Sisters tube station. It doesn't sound much, and is certainly not a name to strike fear into your heart in these enlightened times, but back in the mid seventies, it was one of those places that had gained infamy in the world of the travelling football fan as somewhere near the top of the league of places you were likely to get battered. Keeping my scarf inside my jacket and employing the age-old tactic of walking with my thumbs in a pair of imaginary braces (come to think of it, I might have actually been wearing real galluses) and walking as if was stepping in something unpleasant every time, I passed myself off as a local. Or maybe nobody was really watching me anyway. Whatever, I got to the ground in one piece, which was always a bonus when travelling alone in those days, but it was once inside that the fun almost started.

I did what I normally did back then when I'd arrived at whichever ground the Lads were playing, and wandered about a bit to find my mates. It was only when

I received a hefty kick up the arse that I realised I'd wandered past the non-existent police and stewards and through a gate into the Spurs fans. Perhaps my expression of total shock prevented my assailant from following up his thankfully rather tame attempt at assault, but he just stood there and looked at me. I looked back, evaluated my position both geographically and in terms of survival, screamed some abuse at him, and darted back in to the safety of the Sunderland side of the fence. Having located a couple of familiar faces, we watched our heroes take to the field. The back five was unchanged, with Colin Waldron having established himself as replacement for the injured Jeff Clarke's place after swapping with Shaun Elliott and Mick Coady for a couple of games. Like fullback Mick Docherty, he was one of the unsung heroes of that almost-greatest escape ever, and his performances are one of the reasons I now live in a street bearing his surname. What nonsense, but if there was a Rowell Street in Bishop…

Joe Bolton and Jackie Ashurst completed the defence, while Towers, Arnott, Elliott, and Rowell the midfield and Bob Lee (Bob Lee, Bob Lee, Bob Lee, Bob Lee, Bob Lee…) and Mel Holden (rules the skies) were up front. Spurs had high ideas of themselves, but to me they have spent a lot of time as one of those clubs who are all fur coat and no knickers. Not that I have any particular dislike of them for it, and they've won an inordinate amount of FA Cups and trophy cabinets don't lie, but some of their fans seemed to think that the club was a lot bigger than they actually were. Whatever that means, we at least matched them in the first half, and were entitled to be thinking of at least a point as we hurled abuse across the fence at the home fans during the break. My pre-match opponent managed to catch my attention and impress upon me what he was going to do to me after the match now that he had several hundred mates who would happily join in. I indicated with my fingers how Churchill would have celebrated our impending victory, and left him to his threats. I had several hundred mates with me by then, and a fence with a few policemen standing next to it, so was feeling about as brave as he was. With no goals as we started the second half, we pressed forward and Mel Holden scored the seventh of his eight league goals since Christmas to earn us a well-deserved point. As we celebrated as only football fans can when a draw away from home has been achieved, it slowly dawned on me that I had to get back to Bristol, and preferably without the two black eyes that had distinguished my first visit eighteen months earlier. I had a reputation to live down.

So the scarf went back around my waist under my shirt, and my jacket was fastened up as much as possible without breaking Levi jacket-wearing protocol, and I was off. The Spurs lads had been taunting us with choruses of "It's a long way to Seven Sisters" and it was. It might only be a mile or so, but when you doubted your chances of getting there in one piece slightly less than your chances of not getting a good howking on the platform, it seemed like a lot further. Somehow, I found myself in possession of an orange – there was no room in my pockets for it, I certainly didn't pop in to the local fruiterers and buy it, so it must have been a gift from a mate who thought that I'd be in need of sustenance on my Way Out West. Anyway, I thought I would look very relaxed, and therefore pass off as a local, if I casually peeled and ate it as I walked down the High Road. There was hell on. Sunderland buses were parked on the High Road, and Spurs lads were trying to drag folks off them. Those that they managed to remove were quickly backed up by several who left the bus very much of their own accord, and for a few minutes the pavement was like a rugby scrum, but with a lot more fists and feet flying about. The law eventually intervened, folks who should have been on the buses got onto the buses, and those who shouldn't have been stood over the road and lobbed missiles over the boys in blue and at the buses. There were a number of attempted ambushes on folks who looked a bit Northern, but I got to Seven Sisters in one piece, kept my mouth shut, and eventually the tube came. Thankfully, there were none of the then-frequent interrogations of single young men by the home hoolies which usually started with a conversation asking the time to judge your accent and ended with a flurry of blows and the removal of any colours as trophies. After a fairly simple one-tube into the City, I found myself in the wrong part of Earl's Court on the wrong branch of the District Line – did they run out of colours when building this, the most confusing and complex of Tube lines? Rather than have either two ends or be a circle, this bugger has six possible termini, and I chose the wrong one. Naturally, as Chelsea had been hosts to Forest that afternoon, the respective sets of fans were in the process of knocking seven bells out of each other when I arrived right in the middle of it. I was trying to get back up the down escalator when the Polis came thundering down it, and there was no choice but to go with the flow.

Warring factions separated, I was allowed back up the escalator once they'd been convinced that I was indeed a Sunderland supporter hopelessly in the wrong place at the wrong time, and one of the officers offered to show me where to find the correct branch. The only problem was the eighteen stone Chelsea skinhead he was handcuffed to. Naturally, the officer radioed for assistance in getting the detainee upstairs and to the waiting Black Marias. Obviously a public-spirited sort, Mr Chelsea Skinhead said "It's OK officer, I can find my own way if you're busy."

I got out of their way as quickly as possible, and eventually to Chiswick Park station and thence the Nirvana of the Chiswick Flyover slip-road. Time was getting on, so I took up my position and set my controls for the heart of the sun. There was a car showroom next to that slip-road back then which specialised in top-end sports cars – E Type Jaguars, Aston Martins, and Mercedes Benzes (before Merc became common) and, as I waited for a lift, I fantasised about the imaginary gorgeous young blonde salesperson finishing for the day and offering to take me all the way to Bristol in a Bristol, talking about football and beer, and stopping off in Bath for a posh meal and a few pints. All on her expense account, of course. As it happened, my lifting luck was in that day, but not that far in. A transit, driven by a jolly builder, was going all the way to Bristol town centre, so I was able to save another two pence on the phone call, and spend it on part of the bus fare out to Bedminster Down. An impressive day's travelling, even if I say so myself – two tube rides (three if you included the hiatus at Earl's Court), one bus ride, and a couple of hundred on the thumb. Oh, and a point. Canny.

The fixed penalty meant that I had the dubious pleasure of attending Market Street nick and courts on my return to my Tyneside home to pay off my debt to society. Not a place I hold any great affection for, but at least it raised my street cred amongst the less savoury denizens of some of the town's pubs I used when they recognised me. More importantly, we'd brought a point back from Spurs.

Tranmere

There are occasions in your footballing life when big changes happen, such as when you realise that you're older than all the players, then the manager, then your children get to be as old as the players… well, this was one of those occasions. We had an important game at Tranmere, in that it was the last game of the season and we had to attend. This time, however, the bairns wanted to come as well, which was no surprise. As parents, Pos and I had spent a good deal of our time in bringing up our children in the ways of Sunderland. We'd been taking them to Roker since before they were big enough to go, and we'd just spent a season watching Peter Reid's effective but miserly side batter their way to the top of the Championship.

By the time the final game of the 1995-96 season came around, we might only have scored 59 goals, but we'd only let in 31 and only lost six games. The penultimate game, the week before at home to West Brom, had produced the fourth scoreless game in five, but the point was enough to clinch the championship of Endsleigh League Division One – I bet you'd forgotten it was ever called that – which is exactly what we'd been hoping for all season. Under normal circumstances, which in our case has often been either just avoiding relegation, or actually being relegated, the last away game has always had an extra pull for the fans. We feel sort of obliged to make that extra bit of effort to go there to celebrate salvation, actually witness salvation being achieved, sometimes celebrate promotion, sometimes see promotion being achieved, or in some cases see relegation catch up with us. Whatever the season has brought, it's a chance to let our hair down a bit further than usual and let the Lads on the pitch know that, whatever hand fate may deal us, we, the fans, would always be there to roar them on. On the fifth of May 1996, the twenty third anniversary of that day at Wembley, we had the Championship and promotion to celebrate at Tranmere.

After much discussion over beers in the weeks leading up to the game, Pos and I had decided that there was no reason not to take the bairns with us, and that we should continue their Sunderland education. This might have been one of their first away games, but it was the last game of the season and, as such, an occasion to be respected. So we told them that it was compulsory for Sunderland fans to wear fancy dress at the last away game, and that they'd have to come up with an idea that was suitable for all of us, young and old alike, and preferably something that we could all wear as some sort of theme. Bless their little red and white polyester socks, Kris and Ian came up trumps with the suggestion of Old Fashioned

Footballers – an easy one. They must have been looking at old pictures of Charlie Thompson – that's Charles Bellamy Thompson to you – of Sunderland from 1908 to 1915, and possessor of the most fearsome moustache in the history of the club, and probably football in general. They decided on the long baggy shorts – fine, I'd nicked a few pairs from school which were probably of the Charlie Thompson vintage, and still had them in a box. The shirts were easy, as we all had some "retro" club shirts, with mine being a genuine 1973 nylon oxter-cutter. The socks, big and hairy, were in my case actually my first ever Sunderland socks, and had come as part of my first ever replica kit, which came in a box at Christmas 1962, accompanied by a pair of all-leather (studs and all) boots and a size three caser that took three of my teeth out soon after. Flat caps were easy, and my grandad's miner's kneepads completed the outfit, but the final touch was a collection of Charlie Thompson moustaches, which had taken the best part of a week to perfect. A bit of double sided tape and some Brylcreem, and we were ready to join the party at Prenton Park.

As there were young folk in tow, we decided that, despite it being tradition to ship a few bevies when football celebrations were the order of the day, we'd be sensible adults and drive down and make do with a couple of halves before the match, as we reckoned there'd be plenty of time to get home and make up for lost time after the game. I got in touch with Rob from Uni who lived in Tranmere and had been kind enough to put the kettle on before previous games down there. It was a shame that on one of those previous visits, he had compounded the misery of a 4-1 defeat in the pelting rain by disclosing that he'd gone over to the dark side. I blame myself, as the lad had accompanied me on numerous trips from Jesmond to Roker, and I'd obviously not kept up the preaching when we went our separate ways in 1978. Anyhow, he promised tea and biscuits, gave us directions to his new abode a mile or so away from Prenton Park, and we headed south, west, and beneath the Mersey and found Chez Rob without difficulty. The kettle was on, and not only were there biscuits, but there were sandwiches and fizzy pop. Such splendid hospitality doesn't come free, especially with a Mag, and we soon worked out why. On the customary tour of the new house, we were shown the garden, and more to the point, the biggest hawthorn bush – nay, tree – that I'd ever clapped eyes on. The problem was that it was next to a wall, behind which was a long drop, and its roots were threatening to make the wall collapse and take the garden with it. So it was that one normally dressed Mag, two small girls in Mag shirts, one random relative, and four 1910 footballers with impressive facial hair could be seen heaving on ropes tied to a tree in Tranmere one Sunday morning in May. What the neighbours thought we'll never know, but we tied the thing to some posts and left it at a crazy angle. It's probably long since taken the wall and garden down the hill with it, but who cares – we'd got a free dinner.

Rob walked us toward the ground, and turned back when it became obvious that his daughter's Toon goalie top would not be appropriate clothing. We found the Shrewsbury Arms, savoured our couple of halves as the place filled with fans of both persuasions, and generally got our singing voices in tune. We had been allocated the whole of the new Kop End and all of one side – the crappy old bit that our tickets were for. Never mind, we were there to celebrate, and celebrate we did. Gary Rowell was discovered in the Kop, prompting more than the usual number of renditions of "Gary Rowell World", and the home fans must have felt more than a wee bit inadequate as they tried to bid their team farewell for the close season. The Sunderland sections were packed with pantomime horses, Flintstones, spacemen, numerous Elvises (or is that Elvi?) representing every facet of his career, and, of course four 1910 footballers. We sang, we danced, and we celebrated – but the team just didn't join in, and it was hardly surprising. They'd probably been on the lash since the previous Saturday evening, and the line up was confusing to say the least. Apart from Chamberlain in goal and Craig Russell up front with Michael Bridges, we had Kubicki, Scotty, and Gareth Hall as full backs, and then Bally, Dickie Ord, Lee Howey, Agnew, and Mickey Gray sort of trying to work out where they were supposed to be. When Tranmere were awarded a penalty, John Aldridge put it away, but was left standing in disbelief as the Sunderland fans went wild with delight. What he didn't realise was that there was a match going on between our nearest and nowhere-near dearest neighbours and Spurs, in which they could actually have won the Premiership. Our reaction was to the news that a goal had been scored which buggered up the Mags' chance of the title. I honestly can't remember if it was Man Utd at Boro, or Jason Dozell for Spurs at Sid James Park, but it made us very happy anyway. So we lost 2-0, the fans sang Reidy's name, the stewards tried in a half-hearted manner to kept the gates closed and us in the stands, then the stewards gave up and a joyous rabble of cartoon characters, James Bonds, Elvi (or is that Elvises?), famous military figures, and four footballers (circa 1910) spilled onto the grass. It was all good-natured stuff, Reidy and some players were chaired on shoulders around the pitch, and Tranmere fans shook our hands in congratulation. I'd been given a Sunderland Champions flag by Nige, who'd bought it the previous Saturday in a fit of post-match daftness, and I swapped it with a home fan who gave me a blue Tranmere jumper he just happened to have spare.

We made our way back to the Shrewsbury to catch the end of the Premier League games, and dumfound the locals as we continued to celebrate despite defeat. Of course, the Mags only drew with Spurs, and Man Utd won 3-0 at Boro to win their league by four points, so that huge points lead that had been in the possession of the Barcodes at Christmas had gone. Yeehaa! Another reason to celebrate – silverware, silverware, the Mags have got no silverware, from St James's Park to Eldon Square, the Mags have got no silverware! So we shook hands with the locals again, piled into the car, and made record time (as we seemed to do when driving to or from any ground) back to Bishop, where Pos and I quickly got our respective bairns off to bed, then met up in the Tut to recount tales of the season just gone to anyone who'd listen, and a few who just happened to be in earshot.

is for Villa (Aston)

If we'd used their full name, this chapter would have been just behind Arsenal and we would have had nothing under V at all, so here it stays. We'll skip the 1975 trip, which was memorable mainly for not winning promotion, and being given a good seeing-to by the famous West Midlands Constabulary, and go to the first game of the 1982-83 season.

This was always going to be a challenge - they were, after all, Aston Villa, recent winners of the European Cup, and boasted players such as Withe, Mortimer, and Shaw, but we were the Sunderland Boys, and our team had finished a mighty few paces above the bottom and thus avoided relegation. Avoiding relegation was something we were quite good at, which is just as well, as we needed to do it most seasons back then. In fact, if we didn't go down, we just avoided going down. Maybe an over-pessimistic view, but that was the way it seemed for years. Anyway, we'd ended the previous season with a win over City at home, and when we saw Villa away as the first game, it raised the interest in the new season a couple of notches. Why? Well, we had Wink, and he has a cousin called Sid, better known as Gordon Cowans, and he sorted out a VIP trip for us. He even provided some beer for us at his house on the way down, a tour of the dressing rooms, and a walk on the pitch with the players. This was in the days when the pre-match warm-up consisted of a stroll round the grass, not some poncy, synchronised gymnastic routine and timed sprints and stretches. This enabled us to watch our fans and White Army massing on the terraces, and give a knowing wave to those who were looking at us with that "I know him - who the hell is he?" expression on their faces. As it was the first game, perhaps they thought we were Alan Durban's secret summer signings, the ones above and beyond the only real one, Ian Atkins. At least one of us could have done the job of the recently departed Tom Ritchie, if we were needed.

As we took our seats, the poshest one could blag for nothing, naturally, the teams came out and with Barry Siddall also having left, Chris Turner was number one, with Venison, Munro, Elliott, and Chisholm protecting him. Atkins was the midfield new boy, alongside Mick Buckley, Stan Cummins, and Nick Pickering, with Colin West and a certain Mr McCoist up front. Gary Rowell was on the bench, so our services on the field obviously wouldn't be needed. Well, in our eyes that was a side that could at least put up a fight. For the first half, it looked no more than that, and Mr Cowans did the dirty by remaining the genial host for no more than twenty minutes. After this, he turned all professional, which is what he was paid to do, I suppose, and put the Villa one up. Was he looking for a confrontation at half time, or what? Of course, you don't get to meet the players at the break, even if they did provide the tickets, but the refreshments were top notch, and increased our optimism once more. Our new-found optimism was, for once, rewarded as we produced a much improved performance, and things went decidedly silly as West, McCoist, and Pickering got a goal apiece and give us a bit of a surprise away win at one of the title favourites. As starts to the season go, that was a damn good one. Beating the European Champions on their own patch was a pretty impressive way to get the ball rolling.

As you'd expect, the players' lounge was a good place to be, and I couldn't believe that I was engaged in post-match banter with the likes of the Lord Rowell and Ally Mac, exchanging opinions on how and why we won the game, how the season would progress, and what we'd do in the next few games. Winning just one of the next six didn't come into the conversation, like the last game of that run, 0-8 at Watford. Most importantly, there was a free bar. I impressively beat Tony Morley, supposedly a speedy winger, in a sprint for the last sausage roll, and gave a passable impersonation of a knowledgeable hanger-on during a couple of hours of panic drinking which almost won me my first England cap for ale-quaffing. As someone else had volunteered to drive, it didn't matter, and I could sleep all the way home. Top day – an impressive away win, free beer and food, life doesn't get much better than this. Cheers, Gordon.

is for Watford

In the close season, we'd managed to change divisions without the fuss and bother of promotion or relegation, as the Coca Cola Championship emerged, all fizzy and bright, from the ashes of Nationwide League Division One. Well, that one had us all convinced that the world was a better place. After five wins in the last seven games, we had a right to feel that the season was going our way after a bit of a bumpy start. After what had become something of a tradition – the international break – it was a Wednesday evening game at Watford.

One of the benefits of midweek away games is the arrival of a good excuse for a day off work and a lie-in. That's what most people had done, but I'd gone one better and taken the whole week – a few days in Scotland to catch up with our Gaz at his new Edinburgh base, back home in time for the Watford match. Sorted. This meant that the back seat discussion group were bright eyed and bushy tailed, ready for political and social discussion. The morning's postbag had brought enough interesting nonsense for several hours worth of dissection - the Regional Assembly ballot paper, otherwise known as phase three of John Hall's plans for world domination (phase 1 - knighthood courtesy of the Metro Centre, phase 2 - family's financial future secure, courtesy of the Mags), and a Hibs merchandise catalogue, including Hibernian Chilli sauce. This had arrived thanks to my having bought a pair of tickets from the Hibs box office for the Scotland game there against Trinidad and Tobago, and they pestered me for a couple of years until I rang them to explain that I already had a season ticket, and it was at Sunderland, thank you very much and good luck for the new season. The day's first bonus came when the ticket prices were found to be £5 below estimates, and the second was Rob's new bouffant. Then we hit St Albans. It was my first visit, and it's no wonder, with pubs called the Bell, the Cock, the Old

Cock, the Horn, and the Old Fighting Cocks. We decided we liked the Old Cock Inn the best, but went to Wetherspoon's instead, as we're cheapskates. The usual game of cards played for matches, to be exchanged for the requisite number of 50 pence pieces once back on the bus, as gambling was against the house rules, warmed me up for a wander around the town's older pubs. Not those with the slightly risqué names, of course, and purely in the interests of research.

Clear roads gave us an hour to kill in Watford, where some chose to get "overserved" before kick-off, and then it was into the museum of British football stadia that is Vicarage Road. Sporting the Seven Ages of accommodation in a clockwise fashion from bare terraces, through open seats, a bike shed, a Dutch barn, a dodgy cantilever, that funny thing with the semi-circles on top, and our end – the one with the miniature bogs. Bijou and compact is perhaps the polite way to describe them. We decided to follow recent form down in Elton-land, and concede a sloppy early goal. Neil Ardley hardly ever scored, apparently, but couldn't believe it as our whole defence allowed a low cross to skid through to him, and bang, thank you very much, in it went. Proof, if proof were ever needed, that the best way to break a scoring barren spell is to play against Sunderland. A rare outing for Neill Collins, still filling in for the suspended Breen, alongside Caldwell, and the return of Marcus Stewart and Sleeves Elliott meant that we had a big back line and a lively front line. Surely one of the strangest nicknames ever bestowed on a player, Mr Elliott apparently said "sleeves up" or something similar when trying to ascertain if something was true or not.

We were only behind for five minutes, before we had hold of the game, but we produced few real chances before Watford made a real arse of a free-kick on half way, the ball was passed forward to Elliott, and he showed real composure to pop it away. Oooh, we thought, we can win this, and we piled into them for the next half hour, with Watford still providing the odd break. Level at the break, we should have been more efficient after it. Despite the substitution of Whitley for the more positive Lawrence, chances were restricted to half-decent efforts from Whitehead, Arca (otherwise ineffective) and Stewart. The introduction of Bridges for Stewart was no surprise, but Brown for Elliott was – perhaps it was admission that a draw wouldn't be a bad result, and the chance for the fans to show their appreciation for the little fella, but he'd had have been better left on. As the game wore on, several stud-free moments showed how greasy it was, and the ref did well to let the game flow as much as he did. On the night, it was probably a point won, but we thought that we should be beating teams like this, as they were clearly raising their game when we clearly weren't.

Well, generally disappointed, we trooped back to the bus, watching a nearby firework that must have cost a good couple of quid to put together, and climbed aboard to watch the American police/Hispanic drug cartel swearathon film that seemed to have become compulsory entertainment on away trips. On-screen massacre over, we inflated Lilo Lil mark 3, assumed the crash positions, and indulged in a few hours of freestyle sleeping. I had a few days in Whitby to look forward to. Scotland, Bishop, Watford, Bishop. Whitby. Now that's what I call holiday planning.

W est Brom

There's nothing like a relegation battle to convince you that your presence is essential at an away game, and 1977 was the mother of all relegation battles. From being dead and buried, apparently, at the start of February, we'd gone a bit mad and won a load of games, scoring hatfuls of goals in the process. By the time April came around, we had slowed down a bit, but were still fighting for every point as though our very lives depended on it. Which they did, really...

Games were running out, but we'd brought a point back from Spurs and then drawn at home with Derby, so there was no way I was going to miss the game at the Hawthorns. I'd actually had a car before I left Bishop, but it suffered greatly being used for home games, especially when the roof lining caught fire after one of my passengers messed about with the interior light once too often, and had to be sold for someone else to renovate and love. Being therefore a carless as well as penniless student, and very tight with my cash at the best of times anyway, I decided that a repeat of my hitch-hiking heroics a fortnight earlier was the most sensible option for getting to the West Midlands. Two lifts from Bristol to London and back – this one should be a doddle by comparison. I'd actually been planning this one for a few weeks, and had been in touch with Big Harrier in Liverpool to check that it was a suitable weekend in which to take advantage of my open invitation to visit. I didn't need much of an excuse to dodge a lecture on a Friday afternoon – come to think of it, Friday afternoon lectures were few and far between, probably because a good proportion of my fellow students were of the same inclination as myself. So, there I was at my usual spot at the south end of the Tyne Bridge not long after dinner, hoping to take advantage of the Friday afternoon traffic making its way wherever for the weekend.

As I was actually planning to stay away overnight, I had a bag of gear – I must have been getting all sensible as my 21st birthday approached, as I normally would take inspiration from Great Great Grandad Howe, and stick a spare pair of socks in my pocket if I thought I might get stuck somewhere for a couple of days. Old Joe had emigrated to Virginia with nothing more than a spare collar in his pocket (and his Missus, of course), according to my Grandma, so I thought it only right that I should maintain that particular family tradition of travelling light. Anyhow, the extra baggage didn't hamper my progress, as I was on the outskirts of Liverpool in under three hours, and standing at a bus stop wondering how to get to Toxteth. One of the problems with hitching was that you could get to big places quite easily, but finding someone prepared to give a lift for the last few miles was almost always a problem. Why did my mate's neighbour not decide to pick me up? Did my mate's neighbour even have a car? It didn't matter, as it happened, as I found a bus that passed Harrier's door, and so it was that I sampled the delights of a night out on Merseyside. As it was getting on a bit by the time we'd eaten, it was too late to go into town, so we hit Toxteth.

Jesus. I thought I'd seen some rough pubs off the beaten track on Tyneside and when travelling to away games, but that place was something else. Harrier's local was close by, as locals tend to be, but I was a bit surprised when he led me into the 'Music Room.' I asked what was wrong with the bar, or even the lounge, so he allowed me across the corridor to get the drinks, and look behind the bar into those rooms to see why they were off limits. Well, let's just say that the lounge was inhabited by a different ethnic group than that to which we belonged, and the bar was… I know Boys From The Black Stuff would not make the screens for another five or six years, but the pub in that series could have been based on that room. "Don't make eye contact with anybody but the barman" was the instruction, along with "Don't touch the Tetley's." So I didn't, and we supped our safe beer in the safe room of an unsafe pub. When Britain descended into civil disobedience in 1981, it was no surprise to me that Toxteth was one of the places most heavily featured in the news. Suitably filled with safe beer, we went back to play cards at Harriers, and we spent what seemed like ages talking nonsense to the other inhabitants of the house. They eventually disappeared and I somehow found myself with a real bed for the night. A real bed, with a huge feather mattress, a giant quilt in the days when a tog was part of what kept a scout's neckerchief in place, and really comfortable. I hardly slept a wink, though. Perhaps it was something to do with our earlier conversation, to do with Lord Of The Rings, part of which I had read for the first time after turning in, or something to do with the Lord Of The Rings posters that adorned the wall (scary looking things like orcs and wizards), or something to do with what was on the other side of the yard wall. Toxteth bloody cemetery, that's what, with all its Gothic headstones and spooky trees. Whatever it was, it had my imagination in overdrive all night, so I was in poor form at breakfast.

Such poor form that no amount of persuading would convince Harrier that the match was the thing for him, so I scoffed my toast and went on my merry way. A quick bus ride, directed by someone who lived there, so no problems knowing which one to get, and I was once more off with the thumb. I don't remember how many lifts it took, but it seemed to be going well, and I was chatting away with the driver, when he said that he was going to stop for refreshment. Nothing unusual there, as drivers do that from time to time. I'd even had a half of beer bought by one, so that's what looked to be on the cards as he passed the services and went away from the motorway. I accepted his offer of a half of beer, and then the conversation went more than a little wrong. I won't go into details, as I don't want this to be a top shelf publication, but it quickly became apparent that my acceptance of that drink was considered by 50% of the people taking part in the conversation to be an acceptance of a physical liaison. Oh bugger (sorry, wrong choice of words), how was I going to get out of that one? I was several miles from the motorway, I had no idea if there were any buses, and I had no cash for a getaway taxi. It was also getting closer to kick off, so I couldn't escape in a manner which would knacker my chances of getting to West Brom before three. When the second part of the journey began, my mind went back to a similar experience recounted by Pos from a few years earlier when he'd been propositioned by his lift and had made his escape by jumping out of the car at the A167 roundabout near Aycliffe and hidden in the bushes until the bloke gave up and left the scene. Stotting down the motorway at 70 miles an hour meant that jumping out was not an option, so I decided to persuade him that I'd changed my mind about the match and was going somewhere else. The only problem was that I was stuck in the car, and it was up to him to stop. Thankfully, cars need petrol, so when we did pull into the services and he went to pay, I was off like a shot into the bushes, much to the amusement of the row of fellow hitchers on the exit road. I watched until I saw the car – a brown Triumph Toledo, you don't forget these things if you're planning to use your thumb again – trundle past, with my would-be sweetheart scanning the row of hitchers.

Joining the end of the line, as you did, it didn't take long to get another lift, and guess what? Yes, a Sunderland supporter on his way to the match. Bonus – somewhere to leave my bag as well, Sunderland talk, and the offer of a lift home. For the fourth game in a row, we were unchanged. Siddall, Docherty, Bolton, Waldron, Ashurst, Arnott, Elliott, Rowell, Towers, Lee, Holden. There were 22,000-odd in the ground, the away end was packed fit to burst, and in fantastic voice. I bumped into Sixer, who doubled my options for getting home by offering me a lift as well, and we were off. The team were on fire, carrying on the good form of the last couple of months, and played like they really wanted to win. There have been some cracking games at the Hawthorns in my time – coming from behind to draw 3-3 in 1997-1998, and then coming from behind the following October to win 3-2 spring to mind – but this one is my favourite. The first half was fantastic stuff, and ended up 2-2. The second half was as memorable for the performance of the visiting fans as much as the visiting team. If you've never been amongst several thousand Sunderland fans who sing Ha'way the Lads for fully twenty minutes without seeming to draw breath, then you've missed one of the great sporting events in the world. There's no better feeling, especially when you're away from home and Sunderland score the only goal of the second half to win it 3-2. Fantastic, with a goal from Bob Lee and two, including a nerves of steel penalty, from Tony the Tiger Towers. Another, win, a great atmosphere, and two lifts to choose from - it doesn't get much better than that. I naturally chose the Sixer option for the lift, as, perfectly pleasant as my last lift had been, I would rather sit in a carload of mates in celebratory mood than with a recent acquaintance who might not have understood my behaviour after such a victory. Sure enough, he'd been sitting in the car for ten minutes when I went to reclaim my bag, having not stayed behind for the celebrations that naturally follow dramatic away wins.

So I enjoyed three hours of Sunderland chat and song, and arrived in Bishop in time to pop down to the Cumberland to boast of yet another two points in the bag as we climbed our way to safety. I realise that I'd actually started my journey some twenty five miles to the north, but I could always count on a bed being available at 'home' – that's what parents are for, aren't they? By the time I hopped off the OK Bus on the Sunday afternoon, I'd been away for forty eight hours, spent a night in Liverpool, visited probably the roughest pub I was ever likely to visit, scared myself half to death because of a few posters and their proximity to a graveyard, seen the Lads win away, had a night out in Bishop, oh, and almost become the victim of a sexual predator. All in a weekend's work travelling with Sunderland.

could only be for York... As even we were too young to remember Yeovil.

I t's strange when your derby for the season happens to be at York. A bit like Carlisle – gleefully acceptable in the First (Premier) Division, but hopelessly rubbish when it's in the third. However, this is where we found ourselves in 1988, thanks to the inspired work of Mr Mackemenemy. Still, it's an ideal train trip, being just 20 minutes from Darlo, joyously boasting 364 pubs, no match ticket required, and three points the merest formality. Just turn up, warm up, and be entertained in a late season show of red and white might. We duly arrived in York in perfect time, just before 11 o'clock heralded the opening of the first of the 364 on our list.

Security started early, with Yorkshire Polis videoing every Sunderland fan as they disembarked. Very pessimistic start, but we soon chalked up our daily allowance of liquid as we reduced the "must visit" list to 359. It looked like we would struggle to get round them all, as we entertained Mackems, locals, and bemused tourists alike. Gibba gave us "Alouette", the unexpurgated version, for performance in the presence of over 18s only, Tink "scrunched", which is a very visual display of testosterone which involved a madman running around the pub, and Skinner, Aycliffe's Prince of Pop, provided the coup de grace with two verses of "Lucky Lips" before we were asked to leave. Yet another pub that we henceforth excluded, but there were still another 358 to choose from.

On to Bootham Crescent, a real prefab of a ground, where there was chaos at the turnstiles as the law made a particularly feeble, and potentially dangerous, hand of crowd control. When we did get inside, the famous York Shambles took on a new and frightening meaning. Their idea of safety fencing was that rusty stuff that is used to reinforce concrete. It was rough, it was held up with string, and it swayed about at the slightest touch, it seemed about 12 feet high, and had nasty, sharp, pointy bits sticking out all over the place. People scrambled everywhere to get a view of the pitch, including the TV gantry (sorry, TV shed) and the clubhouse roof, where the police video camera got much better close-ups of the visitors than they had ever expected. I was behind the goal, packed in as tight as I ever remember being in the Fulwell. This was the only occasion I can recall my ability to move and draw breath being dictated by others for more than a couple of seconds. Just as panic began to set in, the local plods saw a bit of sense, and opened a gate to allow the no-man's-land of the main stand, which was noticeably empty, to be filled with a flood of Sunderland fans. Relief. That had been worse than the '75 game when it hoyed down and 4,000 of us tried to get under one umbrella. 8,878 was the official crowd, I'm sure that there were that many in our end alone.

The football was poor, mainly because York hadn't read the script, the cheeky buggers. Maybe they raised their game due to the presence of Denis Smith, John McPhail, Marco, and Viv Busby, all York old boys. We were the big club, running away with the league, and with a massive following. Despite a debut goal from Pascoe, a substitute for the famous Dougie McGuire and a disallowed effort from Gorgeous Gordon Armstrong, they beat us 2-1. McGuire played no more for the Lads, meaning that we'd spent more time in the White Swan that afternoon than he had in a red and white shirt. Smithy had done what managers were supposed to, and bought when the team was winning, with Pascoe coming in. On paper, we were by far the stronger team, with Hesford, Kaysie, Reuben Agboola, McPhail and Benno at the back surely too strong for their attack, and a midfield of Steve Doyle, Armstrong, Owers, and McGuire surely too tenacious and crafty for their midfield. Above all, we had the G-Force. Although still a relatively new partnership, they'd ripped the division to shreds in their first campaign. We even had Frankie Gray on the bench, and the new boy Pascoe. Perhaps it was enough that York felt that they owed Denis Smith one. Whatever it was, it worked for them that day.

We decided on a post-mortem back in town, and managed to evade the visiting "tourists" in Leeds colours lurking in the streets outside our end on our way to pub 358. We decided that we would still walk off with the league, Denis Smith was all right, and Sobs was daft for running the York Half Marathon the next morning on a belly-full of beer (you can't fly the Atlantic without petrol was his reasoning), but we simply couldn't decide on who was the biggest arsehole – Lawrie shit-for-brains Mackemenemy, or Jimmy Hill. Those two seemed to crop up in every such debate, and still do, as few come close to replacing them. In the end we decided on the latter, because he knew exactly what he was doing whereas Lawrie obviously hadn't had a clue. Our increasingly animated discussions had attracted the attention of a couple of females, who stupidly accepted our invitation to join in and give their opinions on the subject. They turned out to be American Psychology students on a course in England, and they'd just found some suitable subjects for their future studies. One looked like Brooke Shields (OK, we'd been drinking a bit, but you get the picture), while the other redressed the balance by looking like Bette Midler. They were obviously top students, as they ponced gin and tonics from us all night. Deciding that it was perfectly normal for two twenty year-old Americans to want to spend the evening in the company of a bunch of (a bit) drunk older men in football colours, we decided to delay our departure. However, free drink was no compensation to Brooke and Bette for putting up with our inane drivel, although they did concede that Mackemenemy (whoever he was) was not a nice man, as they moved on to their next victims.

When we got back to the station we discovered that the last of the regular trains had long since departed, leaving us with a two hour wait for the mail service, the trusty friend of the itinerant, and daft, football fan. This train contained a fair smattering of pissed-up stragglers like ourselves, including the one and only Sammy. There he was, one-time Fulwell legend, scarf round his wrist, and a domino card for every occasion. He informed us that he hadn't seen the game, due to being a victim of police injustice, and muttered something about Harry Roberts, communication chords and Chester-le-Street as he boarded. The last leg for us was a costly post midnight tariff taxi to Aycliffe, ensuring a good old (and expensive) nag the next morning. Suddenly the York half marathon seemed quite a nice alternative.

Well, until such time as Sunderland play in Zagreb, Zaragoza, Zheleznodorozh-nyy, or Zennor (it's in Cornwall and thus a target for pre-season), that's the lot. Adventures will continue even if the alphabet gets no longer, and I'd like to think that every away game in every season produces a tale for some if not all of those who have the good fortune to attend. In case you were wondering where we got such daft names from, they're not so daft, really. Pos is merely the obvious abbreviation of Poskett, so Derek Poskett got Pos (amongst other things) since I can first remember meeting him. Sobs, is merely the slightly less obvious abbreviation of Dobson. When I started secondary school, I had the dubious (mis)fortune of sitting next to someone, because his surname began with a C and mine a D, who insisted on calling everybody by his version of their surnames. His version was arrived at by replacing the first letter with an S, so it's a good job we had no Smiths in our class. So Dobson became Sobson, and, as everyone else's new nicknames were quickly replaced by something more appropriate, mine was the only one that stuck, soon became abbreviated further to Sobs. I've been stuck with it ever since – a plague on Stephen Colley – or should I say Solley.